REAL ESTATE
The Sustainable
Investment

REAL ESTATE
The Sustainable
Investment

STRATEGIES FOR THE NEXT GENERATION

GLEN SWEENEY

& JOHN GORDON

© 2011 by Glen Sweeney and John Gordon

ISBN: 978-1460933381

All rights reserved. Published 2011.
Edited and designed by David Small

For contact information and downloads, visit:
www.thesustainableinvestment.com.

The information contained in this book is for educational purposes only and is considered accurate and authoritative; however, the authors are not rendering legal, accounting or any other professional services and recommend always seeking competent legal and accounting services on any real estate transaction.

For Cooper and Jamie

Contents

The Real Estate Market
What Happened And What Do We Do Now?

- Your investment future, what happened and why
- A social safety net ... *Eat Your Spinach*
- Financial independence
- Wise choices and sustainable investments
- Uncertainty and our investment behavior

Establish Life Leadership Early
What It Means And Why It's Important

- Starts and stops along the way
- The time value of money
- Your life as it might appear on a timeline
- Choices make the outcome possible

What Type Of Real Estate Investment?
And Why Should You Invest In It?

- Decide "why" and then "what" becomes an easier decision
- Farms and forests
- Advantages of starting with residential income property
- Which location and why

When Buying Investment Real Estate, Be Positive But Very Selective
Location, Remember, Location

- Section 1 ... More on why
- Section 2 ... How, careful now
- Section 3 ... Analysis and case studies, forecasting what the future will be like
- Make your experience capital grow

Choosing The Right Partner(s)
What To Do Before You Say "I Do"

- Why have a partner
- What a partnership means
- Your agreement
- Tips that may help

Leverage
Using Debt As A Tool

- What is it?
- How's it work?
- Types of leverage
- The story of a three-legged stool

Management Q & A
Lessons From The Real (Estate) World

- A few stories
- And a little advice

Concluding Thoughts And Beginning Plans

Prologue

They are the baby boomers, the beneficiaries of modern technology and the affluent society it has spawned. But many are now seen as victims of the worst financial crisis since the Great Depression. This Recession (that saw the DJIA down over 50% in 2009) has proven to be a cross-generational experience that includes their children, the Next Generation. These children are now young adults themselves and commonly burdened with debt of their own. They watched (and perhaps questioned their decisions) as their parents dedicated themselves to employers who were obviously not dedicated to them. The Next Generation wondered how so many of their parents' generation could lose work—and hope—as "Enronian" executives managed companies into oblivion and walked away wealthy, rewarded for their failures with golden parachutes. Or, they watched as their parents walked away from their life's work with nothing but broken dreams, not even the means to retire comfortably. All in all, too many baby boomers were lost in the "new normal," a slow, steady shuffle toward lowered middle-age expectations, and now face a much longer life thanks to enhanced technology. As teachers and investors, we had extended conversations contemplating this rather sad story and thought: "What would we tell the post-boomers, the Next Generation, if they were our students?" While we taught in different fields, we noticed our students' critical questions during hard times were basically the same:

What is the best thing to do?
What is the best time to do something?
Who are the best people to work with?

In 1885, Leo Tolstoy wrote a short story about a king who wanted to find the answers to these same questions, which he considered to be the most important questions in life. The king, with all his resources, sought far and wide for the answers, believing this knowledge would give him success in anything he did. But the answers did not come easily, and after a long and frustrating search, the king left his palace in disguise to seek the counsel of a wise hermit. When the king found him, the hermit appeared tired from working in his garden and didn't answer the king's pressing questions. The king offered to do the work, hoping the hermit might rest and provide the answers he sought. The hermit remained silent, however, and the king continued working. From time to time he would ask the hermit again, but received no answers, just more ground to hoe. The king, of course, grew impatient.

One day, a badly wounded man came upon the king and the hermit. The exhausted king helped the man, seeing to his injuries, and soon he began to feel better. The injured man knew the king had left the palace in disguise but recognized him now, and confessed he was an enemy who had come to kill the king to revenge his brother's execution.

The man asked the king, "Why would you help me, of all people?"

"Because you needed help," replied the king.

The injured man begged forgiveness and pledged his loyalty. The king, happy to have made peace so easily, turned to the hermit and tried asking his questions one final time ...

At last, the wise hermit replied.

"You have already answered the questions yourself. The *most important time* is now, because now is the only time when you really have any power to do anything. The *most important people to work with* are the ones you work with now, because no one knows for sure if they will ever again have any dealings with anyone else. The *best thing to do* is 'good' because for that purpose alone was man sent into this life."

In this book, we attempt to answer these questions for you, the Next Generation, in relation to a specific human purpose: Saving and investing *wisely*.

The Real Estate Market

What Happened?
And What Do We Do Now?

WHAT HAPPENED? Investors were deceived, or deceived themselves, into thinking there was reason and accountability in our nation's financial system. The details of this global financial crisis have been played out in the news to the point that it is obvious that this really is a new generation that needs a completely new set of financial guidelines and investment tools, or at the very least, a much better way to use the old ones.

Something about this crisis was different than other recent ones like the recession of the early 1980s, the Savings and Loan scandal or the Dot-Com Bubble. This time our nation's financial system lost more than investors' money: They lost much of what little trust was left. Without trust and a reasonable level of accountability, investors won't invest. Our financial system has damaged its relationship with the individual investor and is going to have a problem attracting them back to the market

1

until trust and accountability are restored. We need to question the cause, not the details, behind the assumptions that allowed this financial crisis and real estate market crash to happen. The details may change from crisis to crisis, but the cause is almost always the same. There is a sickness in the system. The financial losses are only the symptoms. Unchecked greed and lack of accountability are the disease. This means you may be on your own more than you thought and thus need to question your expectations and choices for your personal financial future.

This book is not about how to get rich in real estate, and it certainly isn't about avoiding work or being successful without effort, sacrifice and determination. We can't help you make real estate investments without risk, because risk is the cost of success. We can't even tell you with certainty what will go up in value and what won't. But we can tell you what we think is worth doing, worth restructuring, and why, and in doing so help you avoid becoming a victim of the next financial crisis.

There is a good reason for everyone, but particularly young people, to take their investment future into their own hands. Today's youth may think their world will turn out to be like that of their parents. Pensions and Social Security have ensured that people retiring now at least have a chance at "unconscious affluence" in retirement. Pension plans and government-funded entitlements have made saving for retirement relatively easy for those born early enough. But as we have seen since 2007, the world is changing rapidly. In many ways it is changing so that things will be much harder when people reach "retirement age" or when another recession/depression finds them in a low-paying job or none at all. Even though we are living longer, most people are now taking Social Security as early as possible (62), but receiving much less on a monthly basis. Many owe more than their home is worth, and private company pensions are disappearing at an alarming rate, less than one half of what existed just 30 years ago. The "social safety net," as it's known by earlier generations, is falling apart. We are entering a time of high uncertainty about government spending and a sea of red ink. The Government Accountability Office estimates that entitlements will eat up the entire federal budget by about 2030 unless action is taken to increase taxes or reduce expenditures (now that the "stimulus" and "bailout" spending have occurred and government debt has ballooned, this will likely happen earlier). As we currently accumulate massive debt, we can be equally sure that future interest paid out to service that debt will be an increasing burden.

> **Financial Independence**
>
> The point in your financial life where your money is finally working for you. Your income from your investments has surpassed your income from working and freed you from the financial necessity to work. Many people like their work and will keep at it long after they don't need to just because they find it rewarding, but it's truly nice to not have to.

The case for taking <u>financial independence</u> into one's own hands is convincingly made in the book *Eat Your Spinach* (Gordon and Howard 2006):

> Increasingly, unless people begin to save and invest as early in life as possible, they risk facing an especially bleak later life. "Defined benefit" pension plans (those which promise a given, often generous, guaranteed amount on retirement) are disappearing rapidly. In the best instance, they are being replaced with "defined contribution" plans (those

which promise only income from the money contributed by and for the individual over their working lifetime, but not a definite amount). Most often for new ventures and "restructured" companies, pensions are being replaced with various government-blessed savings vehicles, such as the "401K". These promise long term tax benefits, but are sharply limited in the amount of money that can be contributed to them annually.

Social Security, the perennial "third rail" of American politics, has apparently lost its politically lethal charge and schemes to change (many would say weaken or eliminate) it are proliferating. To take undue comfort from the fact that the Bush administration has backed away from its proposed changes is to underestimate the tenacity of politicians, and to ignore the dire straights into which the federal budget is plunging and the demographics of the future.

Health care costs are rising more rapidly than general inflation and the endless supply of new miracle drugs and treatments are ever more expensive. Partly because of these drugs and treatments, people are living longer and requiring ever more of them. This longer life often includes long periods of expensive nursing care that were rare only 20 years ago.

In the workplace, the lifetime job has become the exception rather than the rule; self-employment is on the rise. On the whole, we think this is a good thing. Self-reliance and risk taking are exhilarating. They lead to thought, effort, commitment and achievement. But they also provide a less sure, if often ultimately larger, income stream than the "steady job" of yesteryear. This means that individuals will need to provide, through savings and investment, for periods of low or no current income.

Finally, as China and India transform into world-class economies, there is no reason to believe that the United States and other "G8" countries will maintain their income edge. It may be that the rising tide of democracy and market capitalism will truly lift all boats. In fact, this is highly likely. But it is also likely that there will be a redistribution of wealth along with trade and productivity so that the relative affluence of the citizens of the G8 countries appears, and is, less. Therefore, just as poverty is often recognized in the comparison with others and not as an absolute, the amount of money one needs to feel included in the "good life" may greatly increase over the life of those now in their teens, twenties and thirties. So far we have systematically underestimated the rate of growth and change in the BRIC countries (Brazil, Russia, India and China). Together they contain well over half of the world's population and resources. To expect them permanently to be denied our standard of living is simple-minded.

All the above reckon without calamity. World-wide depression, Carter-scale inflation, pestilence, bad weather, earthquakes, volcanoes and war often have ruined the prospects of millions. Except for the first two, wealth is not a certain shield from their effects. But, sometimes it is. Fair or not, people with money tended to get out of Nazi Germany easier than poor people. The affluent die at lower rates than the poor in most epidemics of most diseases. It is easier to rebuild your house and life after a hurricane if you have some money. So, a prudent person is financially responsible because there are some events that are relatively predictable (old age, illness, retirement) and because some are not. We are also capable of precipitating calamity ourselves, for example, through government policies. Paul Volcker, former chairman of the Federal Reserve Board, said in late 2005: "I don't know of any country that has managed to consume and invest 6 percent more than it produces for long. I don't know whether change will come with a bang or a whimper, whether sooner or later. But, as things stand, it is more likely than not that it will be

5

financial crises rather than policy foresight that will force the change." [As we write now in 2010, Volcker's likelihood has become reality. The "greatest financial crisis since the Great Depression" is on us.]

For a reasonably apocalyptic but well-reasoned and immensely detailed view of the financial future of those who are now young Americans, you should read, without delay, "The Coming Generational Storm: What You Need to Know About America's Economic Future" by Lawrence J. Kotlikoff and Scott Burns. If you accept their detailed analysis and logic, there is not a moment to lose to begin to prepare for your far financial future.

What Do We Do Now?

The rest of this book is devoted to answering this question. However, the short answer is, not what we did before. Like everyone else, we watched as our economy spiraled downward and investors everywhere saw their dreams and finances in ruins. But even as economies suffered everywhere, not everyone suffered the same. In fact some prospered. What was their competitive advantage? What did they do differently? As we look back now, it's obvious that speculators suffered the most and good managers the least. Investments that made sense were successful and survived; likewise, the investments that failed had red flags and stop signs all over them that we now see clearly in hindsight.

In the past, the strength, integrity and reliability of our financial institutions was sufficient for the individual investor to achieve reasonable results over time. Investment speculation was historically contained by accountability instead of being systemically encouraged by a political, financial, industrial complex that was at best incompetent, corrupt or both. No more. In order to have a high level of success now, the Next Generation (you) will need to be more than passive investors. You will need to be proactive financial managers. Those who are willing, we believe, will have the opportunity of a lifetime.

If we learn from the times and work to achieve sensible investment goals, we can still have a bright future. After all, the old saw says:

> "Good judgment comes from experience,
> and experience comes from bad judgment."

Mistakes tend to be really bad only when we don't learn from them. So we want to share with you some mistakes to avoid and some things to look for in the years ahead.

This book is a guide to making sustainable investments based on wise choices. This book is based on the experiences, research and observations of the authors from an ongoing series of lectures and dialogue. As investors, managers and teachers over the last 40 years, we believe there are current financial issues that need to be better understood, and investment problems that can be easily fixed. We will share a handful of the personal investment lessons we learned early on and some of the tales that make us remember them. We'll share our experience, stories and the tools of our trade that go with sustainable real estate investing from a business, leadership and personal point of view. We believe it is possible for young people to create reasonable investment strategies in real estate to safeguard their financial futures.

One of those things we have taught is leadership. Leadership is most often seen as a subject applicable to organizations, and of course it is. But the concept of leadership, in our view, is even more important in terms of one's own life and establishing "life leadership" early. Making a living and providing for the future are a part of life for everyone. A knowledge of real estate as an investment can be a very important part of leading yourself to a better living and a better future. The skills you develop by actively owning and managing income property carry over into every aspect of your investment behavior and life.

The kind of real estate investing we describe can be done by an individual investor or small groups of investors. Our title is *Real Estate: The Sustainable Investment* because we think the current financial crisis is a chronic, long-term problem that will require long-term changes in our investment management behavior in order to achieve reasonable, long-term results. So much has changed in the last two years that we have trouble recognizing old institutions and ways of thinking. Banks don't seem to want to lend money, which most of us thought was their central purpose, and many people who didn't before have started to save some of their income. Those of us who have survived the financial crisis with some of our goals, dreams and assets intact still want a secure financial future.

We can all take heart from a dose of history. What if it were 1939, the year one author was born? The Great Depression still had the country in its grip and "a third of a nation was ill-housed, ill-fed and ill-employed." Europe was heading into a war that we knew we would finally enter, and our army was smaller than Brazil's. Within two years or so, Japan would sink most of our proud Pacific Fleet in one attack. We rose to those challenges. The ones facing us now ought to be relatively easy to confront.

The contradiction here, of course, is that the United States is slowly emerging from the worst recession since the Great Depression. In addition we are in the midst of one of the worst real estate markets in our history, all caused by a mortgage crisis of unprecedented dimensions. Why would any rational investor even consider real estate now? All the reasons to invest in residential income property are the same as they were before the current financial crisis. The only difference now is that prices are lower, interest rates are lower, and it's a buyer's market. Plus, you don't have nearly as much competition over any given property you may wish to buy. Basically, it's an extraordinarily good time to invest (wisely) in real estate. In fact, including it in your long-term plans has become more critically important than ever.

Of course you're worried that the property may still go down in value after you buy it. As events have proved, it may well do that. In the short term, that may be out of your control; in the long term, which real estate investing is, there probably isn't too much to worry about. Remember the two things your parents and grandparents said you could be certain of? Death and taxes! Considering the current deficit, it would be foolish to bet your future well-being that taxes will go down. So in the long term, either the currency will be worth less or the asset will be worth more. Either way, your real estate investment is likely to be part of a chain that keeps pace with inflation (and the economy). That's why there probably isn't too much to worry about.

However, two issues regarding financial decision making are as critical to your investment success as the performance of your investments: 1) Your emotional performance; and 2) Timing in how you deal with doubt and perplexity. Both timing and performance as they relate to investing are often rationalized instead of being rational. After looking at our graph of investment behavior (p. 11), you'll see the emotional problems created by the discomfort of investment uncertainty (called <u>cognitive dissonance</u>, or buyer's remorse). But we think we can help you overcome your concerns and discomfort. What is really different now is that the opportunity of a lifetime may be right in front of you. A good leader seizes opportunities and does so quickly. All leadership includes the understanding of taking calculated risks, and real estate investing is a journey that does as well.

Cognitive Dissonance

What often happens because it's easier to change our mind than our behavior. Cognitive dissonance can be explained as the emotional discomfort of having made a decision and being left with feelings of uncertainty and buyer's remorse (or even sour grapes). Cognitive dissonance is reduced after a decision by positive evidence that the correct decision was made. Likewise it is increased if there is negative evidence about the decision and will be rationalized by justification or behavioral change. Remember: It's always easier to change liquid assets than it is to change fixed assets, and that may be your one good reason why it's not always a good thing.

Consider these points carefully:

Distressed Pricing
Prices have dropped significantly in attractive locations.

Low Interest Rates
Interest rates have not been this low in years.

Availability of Property
Residential income property is a long-term investment, and there is more of it available at better prices right now than there has been in years. In addition, there is a real

lack of reasonable alternatives for reaching your long-term financial goals.

Risk

The greatest risk is to do nothing and to fail to build wealth while the opportunity exists. Other risks can be estimated and priced. It may help to think of risk as the cost of opportunity, so the "do nothing" risk is financially fatal. You probably will not gain wealth without some risk, but you can reduce risk with work. When you understand the work required to be successful, you can reduce uncertainty.

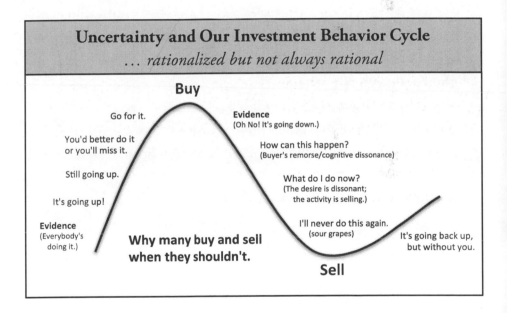

Caveat Emptor ... Let the Buyer Beware

The more difficult an investment decision seems to be, the more anxiety and doubt it tends to create, both before and after the purchase. Prior to an investment this causes procrastination, and after the investment this causes cognitive dissonance or buyer's remorse. This explains why many investors will often join the herd mentality. They follow the excitement of an upward investment trend and buy at or near the top of a market, only to follow the doubt back down, panic, and sell at the bottom.

Difficult investment decisions also tend to have perceived opportunities but increased complexity, making it difficult to move out of our comfort level or equilibrium. What this means is no change = no regret = no investment. We duck the information overload but miss opportunities. So in order to take advantage of the opportunities, we put ourselves in line to deal with the cognitive dissonance or buyer's remorse and the discomfort of the conflict we experience: "Did we make the right decision?"

Usually, evidence that you did the right thing reduces the conflict. If the market for whatever investment you bought continues to improve, you have reduced your conflict. However, the market didn't improve because you bought at the top! So the evidence proves you made a bad decision. To make matters worse—in effort to reduce the cognitive dissonance—you will undoubtedly sell, probably at or near the bottom. Don't feel bad. This is "normal," but it really makes it hard to get any investment traction.

Think of the investment cycle on p. 11 as just one wave in a series of many. The waves go up and down and never stop. Imagine a small, light boat caught between those waves. It would be unstable, right? Now think of a boat large enough to span the individual waves and ride across them, instead of going up and down with each one. Your liquid assets are the small boat and your long-term investments (fixed assets) are that large boat. Experts often argue for diversification with liquid asset investments. We do as well, but we also strongly argue for diversification into fixed asset long-term investments, such as income property. Most people will never make any long-term fixed asset investments, and you can see what boat they are in.

Because your emotional desire is always to perform at an optimal level, it will usually give you the worst possible investment result. *So*, grasshopper, make your investment decisions based on your analysis, *not* only your feelings.

As you see, if the opportunity exists, then the time to lead is now. As promised, we will tell you stories from our experiences and give you strategies to invest and manage wisely, but only you can decide if you are ready for a change, an entrepreneurial change where you become responsible for your own success. Change can often involve a kind of risk that isn't financial. Frequently, as we showed you in the investment cycle, cognitive dissonance involves the emotional risk of giving up what you have and where you are right now in exchange for the uncertainty of what might be. But if you really don't like the way your investment future is shaping up now (many don't) and you are ready to change it, then what are you really risking? The answer is nothing! Statistically, you are on a bridge to nowhere and giving up nothing in exchange for a realizable and very good dream.

You know you can figure out how to do this, how to come up with that down payment on a small non-home property somewhere. Everyone does for their first house, why not for your second? If you think you can't, we can show you how. This book isn't just a road map with easy directions, it's a navigation system to financial independence and will guide you where you need to go and show you how to get there. It's normal to dislike change, but change is necessary when you want a better outcome. Even if you know little to nothing about investing in real estate, you probably already know that your tenants will, in fact, make the vast majority of those mortgage payments, and that in not too many years that property will be paid for. At that point the asset is yours and those payments will go to you for the rest of your life.

What we think we have learned is that the obstacles will be the same and that almost anyone can be a successful real estate investor by combining hard work with several fairly simple concepts. But the sort of investing we are describing here is any-thing but a "get rich quick" scheme (if it seems too good to be true, it is too good to be true). This kind of invest-ing requires study, commitment and, well, we will say it again, hard work.

"If you don't know where you're going, any road will take you there."

Before we describe those concepts and the work that must go into them, we urge you to think about why you might invest in real estate or, indeed, any other assets, ranging from savings accounts to growth stocks. What is your goal? What is your dream? For many of us that dream, that goal, is financial inde-pendence. What is it for you?

Good leadership always starts with a vision. In this sense a vision is not a vague urge to achieve something good; it is a definite future you can see and describe. One of our favorite leadership aphorisms is: "You can't predict the future, but you can create it." Your vision for investment, including real estate, should not only include your financial goals and means to achieve them, it should fit realistically into the rest of your life.

If you are under 40, or are concerned about the next 30 years, you should read this and similar books very carefully be-cause it isn't certain that your employer or your government will provide for your retirement. Investing in the right real estate the right way (along with a balanced set of other investments) can and will, if you work hard at it. Remember: Only by saving and investing carefully can the young of today be assured a comfortable, or even tolerable, financial future.

2

Establish
Life Leadership Early

What It Means
And Why It's Important

LIFE LEADERSHIP (leading your life) effectively means building a life rich in all those things money can't buy *and* having the financial independence to enjoy them. To establish life leadership, the first step is to see your life "as a whole." Part of this is to see that making or having money isn't everything, but it is a necessary and unavoidable part of the picture. To have security, self-confidence and a positive outlook, you need a viable financial plan to keep and invest some of the money you make (or inherit, if you're lucky). The Great Recession we are now recovering from—we hope—has presented us with unusual investment opportunities and difficult investment choices. However, there are always abundant opportunities for those ready to move ahead.

A Tale of Getting Started

John started investing in real estate when he was a relatively young professor. With guidance from Glen, who was teaching Finance at the same university, he bought a duplex and then an eight-plex (with another investor), which he managed himself. He and his wife had the discipline to maintain these modest investments through some fairly difficult financial times. One of the characteristics of all good leaders is discipline. Becoming a disciplined saver and investor is another step toward creating a good life for yourself and those you care about. When John sold those buildings, some years later, the money helped put his son through Yale.

The aggregate events of people's lives are as various as fingerprints but have broad similarities with respect to money and investing. You are faced with a very basic choice about your money and your relationship with it: Work for your money the rest of your life, or make your money work for you. At the point when your investment income equals or exceeds the income from your occupation, you have reached what is referred to as financial independence. So you either lead your money, or your money leads you. Now, you may already be shackled to a job by "golden handcuffs," but if you want a "golden parachute," you are likely going to have to make your own. We don't recommend waiting for someone else to give you one. Essentially, the eventual outcome of life leadership is your prerogative. Lead or follow. Do something or don't. Your decisions now will determine that eventual outcome.

Building a better financial future and achieving financial independence is like building a house. When you build a house, you usually start with a plan, which is followed by a series of decisions (based on that plan) to arrive at your goal—a safe house you can live in and enjoy. You begin your financial planning process by understanding the time value of money. Without this understanding, your plan will have no foundation. Basically, this means understanding that a dollar at some point in the future is not worth as much as a dollar today. That's because dollars, like brains, are supposed to be working. The longer one (or both) of these are working, the better off you should be.

The Time Value of Money

To get us started, here are a few terms regarding the time value of money, as explained in *Capital Budgeting: An Individualized Curriculum* by Glen R. Sweeney.

Present Value (PV) is the amount you have now, today, to save or invest. (Notice we didn't mention spend. That's because you, like most of us, won't need any help at all with that.)

Future Value (FV) is how much that amount you have today, **PV**, will be worth in the future (**t** or **N**) *if* you save or invest rather than spend. Most won't. But if you're different and you do save or invest, you can factor in another variable: your interest rate (*i*), or growth rate, which shows how much your **PV** increases annually. This also shows how much any given **FV** must be discounted by to yield a valid **PV**.

Now let's look at a couple of simple examples using the concepts **PV**, **FV**, **t** and *i*.

Let's say you put away $1,000 and left it for 10 years at 10%. Ignoring taxes and a few other minor things, you would have about $2,594. The $1,000 is your **PV** and the $2,594 is your

FV. Similarly, $2,594 ten years from now—discounted to the present at an *i* of 10%—is worth $1,000 today.

An interesting way to look at **FV** is to think about how long it takes to double your money. One easy way to estimate this is with an experience-based technique we call "the rule of 72." This works by dividing 72 by the interest rate (stated as a whole number) you are able to earn on your investment. For example, .10 becomes 10. Divided into 72, that gives you 7.2, a close approximation of how many years it will take to double your money with 10% interest.

To find out how long it will take to double your $1,000 from the example above, take 72 and divide it by the 10% you're receiving as interest. So, 72/10 = 7.2. You would double your money in 7.2 years.

Next, let's say you start now and put away $1,000 every year for 10 years. Here you are calculating the sum of an <u>annuity</u> (a stream of fixed payments over a specific period of time). Still earning 10% interest, you would have about $15,937 at the end of 10 years. Now, if you were to continue this for 30 years, you would have about $164,494. Hey, this could be good, right? Wrong! $165,000 socked away at today's rate of about 3% is only going to earn $4,950 a year *and* you still have to pay taxes on that. Remember: Financial independence means you have enough to live on at the level you are used to living *or better*. Most likely $4,950 isn't going to cut it.

Another problem with reaching your goals through savings is that you have to put money in the bank and *not* touch it. Most of us won't or can't do this. And if we can, even for a while, we'll eventually give up (or worse, take all of it out for an emergency or just something we think we need, and spend it). Of course we promise ourselves we'll start saving again soon. Sounds like dieting, doesn't it? There is so much fuzzy thinking when it comes to finance and investing. The truth is things happen—life happens and comes at you fast—and your best efforts at saving can be easily thwarted.

This doesn't mean you shouldn't save. Saving is a great way to put something away for emergencies and to build the cash you need to make other investments. Saving alone, however, is *not* usually a good or efficient way to

Annuity

Any recurring payment can be considered an annuity, such as Social Security payments, payments on a contract, or rental income from an investment property that is paid off. According to an article in the *Wall Street Journal* (December 17, 2010), saving enough to purchase an annuity with annual increases to replace Social Security income is a virtual impossibility for "most" Americans. Isn't it odd then that "most" Americans can figure out how to buy a home, which becomes their best investment, yet will spend the rest of their lives unable or unwilling to buy a second one, which would provide an annuity income for the rest of their lives (i.e., retirement)?

become financially independent. What saving does do is create liquidity—financial jargon for having enough cash to respond quickly to problems and take advantage of opportunities—and is therefore critical to your financial security and your financial success.

Liquidity is also an excellent measure of how well your investments are working. You'll know better than anyone how much your investments are hurting if you're not liquid. Most planners recommend you have half of a year's worth of living expenses in a savings account, where it is easy to access in an emergency. As a survivor of this last recession, hopefully you

Liquidity

A general measure of how easily an asset can be converted to cash to meet current obligations. In business, this is a common measure of a business's financial well-being. The problem of liquidity, when it comes to individuals, is that too often everything is liquid and everything is lost or spent (as we are unfortunately seeing in this current financial crisis). In business, a common ratio used to measure a reasonable amount of liquidity is called the "current ratio," which is the ratio of cash (or cash-like assets) to current obligations. As long as the company can easily meet its current obligations, it's free to invest in less liquid assets that will have a higher return and help magnify the profit of the company, which is its responsibility to the owners/shareholders. We have this same obligation to ourselves and families—to have safe and sufficient liquid assets but also to invest in less liquid assets that will help ensure our future success.

noticed that one of the biggest problems with the management of liquid assets is asset allocation. <u>Asset allocation</u> refers to the decision mix you have used in making investments: cash, stocks, bonds, real estate and others. Liquid assets are considered "safe" assets. In financial terms, safe means low risk, convertible to cash and guaranteed by the full faith and backing of the United States government. Therefore only two types of truly liquid assets exist: cash in an FDIC (Federal Deposit Insurance Corporation) insured bank account and federal government bonds. Even federal government bonds can fluctuate in price, however, depending on markets and interest rates, so the term of the bonds becomes critical if they are to be considered liquid. Stocks, for example, are liquid but not always safe, as we have clearly seen in this recession, where they have sometimes gone

Asset Allocation

Basically the idea of not keeping one's eggs all in one basket. Investing in different asset classes reduces the risk of unacceptable loss by spreading the risk across uncorrelated investments. Just because one investment does poorly, the other may still do fine, thereby balancing your return. However, the term is usually only used for making investments in liquid assets. The investments are allocated only between similar, and usually current, assets. Two problems with this type of asset allocation are:

First, as history indicates, most Americans will never get enough assets to realistically generate income sufficient for anything close to what they will eventually need for financial independence.

Second, the evidence of a beginning investor's success shows no real long-term proof of benefit for active secondary management of their investments (maybe because of fees). Look no further than the hedge funds of 2006 that were routinely charging 2-20. That means they were taking 2% for management and 20% of your gains as a bonus. Most of those hedge funds are gone now, along with much of their client's money. In addition, turning over all responsibility for your investment success may leave you with no real money management skills of your own.

Our central argument of this book is about "life leadership" and asset allocation for diversification into fixed asset investments (small income property being an easy, entry-level example) for an improved and balanced long-term result, as well as the development of real (money) management skills.

to zero. As Will Rogers said, "I'm interested in the return on my investment, but I'm even more interested in the return of my investment."

So although stocks and bonds are convertible to cash, they are definitely not risk free. As we have seen, they can and do go down just like the real estate market. And when both markets go down at the same time, the result can leave you with nothing. Many people lost perfectly good investment properties because they thought their investments in the stock and bond market were their source of liquidity. You will find countless examples of individuals who appeared to be very successful but didn't have sufficient liquid assets when they were needed. When the markets went down, they lost what didn't have to be lost, because they didn't have enough cash to make it through the hard times.

> *The borrower becomes the lender's slave.*
> PROVERBS 22:7

Hard times are guaranteed in business, yet the results are almost always considered a surprise (or circumstances beyond our control). For this reason, liquidity is even more important when you're investing in income-producing real estate because, by its very nature, a real estate investment is illiquid. Another word for *hard times* in the income property business is *vacancy*. Higher than expected vacancy means less cash flow, and that means you have to make up for it with cash reserves. Imagine needing cash and finding out it's not there. For example, it's easy to forget the need for liquidity when you find a great investment opportunity. You eagerly invest but end up stretching yourself too thin, only to find that when an emergency happens or hard times come, you can't survive.

A Tale of Liquidity
No Hard Feelings

One of my (Glen's) very first real estate partnerships went from boom to bust just for this reason—lack of liquidity. The partnership was doing fine. We owned a nice apartment building in a great location. The economy was good but starting to go into a recession. Then my partners moved far away and, because of the distance, said they wanted to sell. I was the managing partner, but they had the deep pockets and the controlling interest in the partnership. I found a buyer for our apartments and had it under contract—at a great price. We all would have done well, but my partners wouldn't agree to the terms, which involved carrying a loan for some of the purchase price. The deal fell apart.

This wasn't the primary problem, though. The real problem was that we had a big loan on the apartment building and were making regular capital contributions to the partnership. After this deal fell through, they stopped making theirs! I was in a very bad situation. I tried to pay the mortgage and operating expenses for the apartment building, but couldn't make it with just the operating income from the apartments. It was an awful position to be in, and I can truly relate to the people who are now losing their homes and investments in this recession.

My partners took advantage of the situation and bought me out for next to nothing.

"It's just business," they said. "No hard feelings."

No hard feelings? I lost all the money I had put into this, all I could have made, all the work, *and* felt like I had been cheated. But I also learned something: Be careful with leverage, partners and your partnership agreement. Don't put yourself in a negative cash flow business where you are dependent on capital calls to meet your operating expenses and you don't have control of the capital. When you have a positive cash flow and liquidity, things are always easier to sort out.

But this story isn't over.

We had bought the apartment building for about $250,000. The offer my partners rejected was for $350,000. After they bought me out, they tried to sell the building on their own, initially offering it for about $450,000. They tried and they tried and they tried to sell it over the next few years, lowering the price each time. Now the recession was at its low point. They were living out of town, not getting along with their property manager, had vacancies, and were desperate to sell. One day I drove by and saw a huge sign out front offering it for $165,000. I called the realtor and said to be sure to tell them who the offer was from, but if there were no "hard feelings," I would give them $160,000 cash. They took it. Today the apartment is full and worth (as you might suspect) quite a bit more. No hard feelings!

Your Life in "Parts"

Before we go on about the need for financial planning, independence and investing in real estate for *you*, the Next Generation, let's make this personal. Think about why your investment

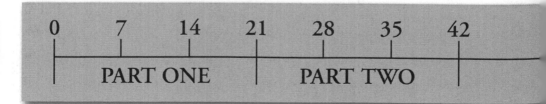

decisions are important. Take a look at your current life, your past, and your future. Draw a timeline from zero to however long you hope to live, and divide it into four meaningful parts, each with segments of 7 years, like the example below. Think of this as your life, from birth on, divided into 7-year sections and put on a line. Remember the rule of 72 for doubling time? That's why we are using 7-year segments. Get a 10% return and the doubling time for your investments will be about every 7 years, but ... let's see how you do.

Part One ... "Youth"
In this first part, from 0 to 21 or so, you really can't be expected to do too much in the way of investing or saving. You just got here; you're young, broke, dumb, but hopefully getting educated or learning a trade. There is not much extra money here, and you're probably in love and need a better car.

Part Two ... "Young Adult"
From 22 to 42 looks more promising. This is where you start your career. At first the pay is not great and the hours are long, but that will change in time and you'll be doing much better. Of course, this is the time when you'll probably be getting married, unless you were a little hasty and got married in Part One (but let's not go there). Now that you are married, Congratulations! Hey, two incomes. This could be really good. Did you hear

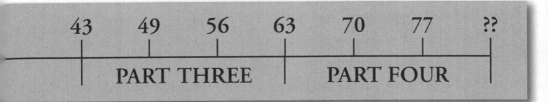

anything about this possible subprime mortgage crisis and re-cession on the news? Don't worry, it probably won't be that bad.

Now you can really start to save and invest. Maybe you should get a house first, though. Go ahead. Stretch your bank account a bit. Get a good one. You have two incomes, and it can only go up in value, right? You're both scheduled for raises real soon too. What's that? She's pregnant? Hmmm. Oh well, back to one income for now, but you'll make it. This isn't as easy as it looked, is it? Maybe that variable-rate mortgage and small down payment on the house you really couldn't afford wasn't the best idea after all. Seems like those payments are going up every month, doesn't it? Almost forgot those school loans. And wouldn't you know it … now that second car needs tires. Not just tires, they say? Brakes, shocks and alignment too?

Don't worry. If we don't do our real estate or other investing now, there's always Part Three. By the way, your wife called. She needs a root canal *and* she's pregnant again. Congratulations!

Part Three … "Middle Age" (Already? Is that possible?)
Now this section—from 43 to, oh, about 63—should be a good one for investing and will take you right up to the age where you can collect your Social Security (if it's still there). You seem to have survived the recession so far, you have a good job, a couple of kids, a few weird pets, a boat, a time share, two car loans, a small balance on your credit cards that you intend to pay off very soon, and a second mortgage. All you have to figure out now are vacations, braces, sports, private lessons in some-thing, weddings soon enough, and why your boss is in your way—stuff like that. You say you're exercising enough? Eating right? Isn't it cute how the dentist can put numbers on your receding gum line now? Have you had that first colonoscopy?

Can you believe how much college costs these days? Wait, you do have that figured out, don't you? Kids sure grow up fast. You say you're not going to buy them a car? Good move. Make them do it on their own and learn the value of money. That's great … and they can always ride around on their friend's motorcycle until they do.

You know you really need to sit down some night and get to work on this financial planning and investment stuff. Get it going, you know? Bought a book on investing, did you? Very good! Isn't it interesting how pretty much everyone buys a house and it becomes their best investment, but they never buy another one? Hmmm. You'll be different, though. How many are you going to buy? Ten, you say? I always think 10 is a good number. You know, like, yeah, I've got my 10 rental houses, and I'm glad I got them when I did.

What's that? Your wife had an affair with the yoga instructor. She's leaving you and wants what? She wants how much? Is she crazy? And the dog is really sick. OK. This is bad, *and* you have more toys than investments. Here's a little free advice: Sell the boat! If you're thinking of getting remarried any time soon, don't. Instead, just walk down the street, find a woman you don't like at all, and buy her a house!

Oh well, there's always the next section of your life.

Part Four … Hmmm, enough said?
In Part Four of your life—from about 64 to only God knows when—the kids are grown and gone, along with your ex-wife and at least half of everything you used to own, except for your house, which belongs entirely to her. Funny, the only thing she still needs from you is money. You say you lost how much on your 401K? Ouch! That's almost as bad as you did in the stock

market, isn't it? Well, look at the bright side: She gets less! You say you heard she moved the yoga guy into the house. Wow, that must really piss you off! Too bad they won't get married and make the alimony stop. That is some car he has, isn't it? She even got the Christmas ornaments your mother left you? That is really bad. You have to give her credit, though, she sure had a good attorney. But on the positive side, you can finally get started with that investing. Hey, she didn't take your copy of this book, did she? Oh, by the way, you're out of sections. It's amazing how soon "not now" can become "never."

You might be thinking this summary of your life is mean and cynical, but in fact it isn't. Everything we wrote about happens—and it happens a lot. It's called bad timing, personal circumstances and procrastination. That's why we can laugh about it. The financial outcome of what happens on your life line is your prerogative. All the negative things we included are actually the lightweight problems of life. We left out the heavyweight problems, some of which you will probably have to face and overcome—death, loss and grief, physical and mental illness, natural disasters and acts of war, crime, accidents and addictions that destroy everything in their path, alienation of loved ones and the loss of friends. We left out all the real serious pain of life and ageing that happens every day to people everywhere. This rather incomplete list of what we left out—when added to the everyday neglect of our finances and other stuff that happens on that life line—illustrates how difficult it can be to achieve your financial goals.

Does this mean it's not worth doing? Does this mean it can't be done? No, it means that if you don't know where you're going, any road will take you there. It means you didn't plan to fail, but that you failed to plan! You neglected your money.

People come to this country every day, enduring unbelievable personal and financial hardships, not even speaking our language, for the chance to make their financial outcome their prerogative. They come for just that—the *chance* to have a say in their outcome, the same chance we are all guaranteed. By the time you reach Part Four, you'll have dozens of stories about your life and the chances you had. Will they be about your financial planning and real estate investments? Will they be stories to follow or stories of what to avoid? Will they be success stories? It's up to you. But they certainly won't be if you don't do any financial planning or make any investments. Sure, things in life can go against us (and they will), but as the prayer says, we need the "courage to change the things we can."

We need to like those things that are good for us, like dieting, exercise and investing. Wouldn't it be great if we only liked and ate food that was good for us in an amount that was reasonable? Or if we were so passionate about exercising that we actually looked forward to it? If a balance in diet and exercise is the right thing to do, then so is a balanced investment plan.

Life leadership, planning for your future, and planning your investments can give you the financial outcome to make you rich in the things money can't buy ... and give you the financial success to enjoy them. Investing in income-producing real estate is now more than ever an important part of this equation. Part of the reason real estate investment has become more important is because of control. As the saying goes, "It's not what you make, it's what you keep and control." Investing in real estate gives you control. It's like Monopoly in real life, and you can play if you want to. Now that sounds like something you can learn to like, doesn't it?

Recall that example of $1,000 saved or invested at 10% as an annuity, where you saved $1,000 per year for 10 years. Imagine that instead of just saving, you bought a few five-acre lots ten years ago for about $20,000 apiece, each with $1,000 down and a monthly payment of about $100 a month. Eventually you sold one of those lots for $185,000. That's about 10 times better than you could have done with just saving. Why? Because of leverage, financial leverage. You see, it wasn't the $20,000 that grew to $185,000. It was the $1,000 you used for the down payment on that lot and your commitment to the investment to pay $100 a month while it did its thing. You can find deals like this if you're willing to look; we did.

Life leadership is about adapting to change and is only easy when the decisions are easy. Important decisions are always tough, and decisions about buying property are important. Most people won't make the decision to invest in the lot, the rental house or the small apartment. They won't make the investment even when they could have. There is a natural caution about making positive choices, even after careful study to make the investment. This must be overcome. There are far too many reasons "why not" to list and examine. But chances are, regrettably, that someday they will ride by a lot, rental house or small apartment they could have invested in and say, "You know, I could have bought that back in …" Life leadership is about critical thinking and making those hard decisions when you have the opportunity, so *you* don't become *them*.

Imagine you are thinking of buying a new SUV and getting rid of your old car, even though it still runs fine. Your budget for the new SUV is $40,000. While reading through the classifieds for cars and SUVs in your local paper, you see an ad for someone selling five-acre lots for $20,000. They only ask for

$1,000 down, and they will carry a contract for 30 years with 5% interest.

You start to wonder, "Isn't that the area they say that new resort is coming in and is growing at 10% or more a year?" This could be a smart investment, but you would just look so good in that SUV. What would happen if you bought some of those lots (instead of buying the SUV) and they appreciated 10% a year?

Let's compare:

YOUR PURCHASE	COST	CASH DOWN	MONTHLY PAYMENT (*i* & t)
New SUV	$40,000	$4,000	$679 (5% for 5 years)
Land (2 lots)	$40,000	$4,000	$193 (5% for 30 years)

In 10 years, your new SUV will be a piece of junk, and you'll be lucky if it's worth $4,000. Your lots, by appreciating at 10%, could be worth approximately $104,000. Even more interesting is that you could have done both. Your payments on the SUV were $679 a month, and your payments on the lots were only $193. You could have purchased the lots, paid your property taxes, and still had money to buy a less expensive car. (FYI, those lots would be worth almost $700,000 in 30 years if they appreciated at 10%. By that point, your SUV would be a distant memory and probably worth nothing. The lots may or may not go to $700,000, but they will probably be worth more than an old SUV.)

Yes, there is the big question: How do I find those lots? The answer? You have to start looking! You must *have* something you are looking for, something you are willing to try and invest in over the long term. The future is not ours to see, my friend. We don't know with certainty what will go up or down in value (but we have a strong hunch that the value of a dollar will go down ... and you do too). We do know that if you buy income-producing property in a good area (one you know well and believe will appreciate), it will probably be worth something someday, especially if you are confident it will out-perform the market. A key point here is that you think long term, manage your property well, pay it off, and keep it until you can move it into something better.

Likewise, if you don't buy anything (statistics say you won't), you will have nothing! That is guaranteed! In fact, we are so confident in everything we are telling you that if you try it for the next 30 years and fail, we will return the money you spent on this book. Just don't lose your receipt.

Now we have a question for you: Do you recall **PV**, **FV**, **t** and *i*, and how to use them? If you don't, it's fine, but we have a suggestion. Buy a good financial calculator (usually less than $100) and figure out how to use it immediately. The HP 12C is a really nice calculator for almost any financial need you may have. You'll notice the **PV**, **FV**, **t** and *i* functions right away and will quickly learn to use them in your mortgage calculations.

Let's review your options:

> **<u>Option #1</u>**   Do nothing.
>
> **<u>Option #2</u>**   Buy this book and put it on your shelf.
>
> **<u>Option #3</u>**   Buy this book, study the ideas, study our stories, look for other stories, get a mentor, have a dream, make a plan, and then put your plan into action.

Option 3 is a small but very good part of your financial life, or pattern of investment behavior. We call it Effective Life Leadership. Just remember not to let the *good* parts get in the way of the *best* parts.

What Type of
Real Estate Investment?

And Why Should You Invest In It?

THE TYPE OF REAL ESTATE INVESTMENTS you make to get started depends largely on your personal situation, but also on your personal preferences. You can narrow your options down by first answering the second question in this chapter's title: "Why should you invest in it?" The answer is not always obvious or easy. When you make an investment in property, it's almost always:

1. A long-term investment made for long-term capital appreciation for the purpose of building net worth and wealth.

2. Because it has or will soon have income sufficient to service all debt and expenses for the duration of any debt on the property, and make a return on any invested

capital. There will also be a reliable income stream after the property is paid off.

3. To diversify your asset allocation to include fixed (non-liquid) assets and leverage.

4. To take advantage of tax strategies such as <u>depreciation</u>, capital gains, sheltering other income and tax free exchanges (1031 ... look it up).

Depreciation

An important consideration when investing in income property. The idea is that you are allowed to expense out over the life of the rental property the cost of the property for a period of 27.5 years. The reality is that for the most part any property in good condition and in a good area will in fact appreciate over those years giving the owner a source of extra cash. There is considerable disagreement over this in academia but the fact of the matter is that if the property appreciates and you save money on taxes at the same time then depreciation is a source of cash and you need to know what it is because it's part of your return on the investment.

5. To have an investment that is legally protected—you have a deed. You may also have other legal rights, such as "first right of refusal" on related property or the right to borrow against your equity in the property.

6. Because "They aren't making any more of it!" an observation made by Will Rogers, which definitely does not apply to the investments in the top part of your balance sheet. (Think about this: They "make" everything in the top part of your balance sheet: cash, stocks, bonds,

Collateralized Debt Obligation (CDO)

A generic term for a form of asset-backed securities—including Collateralized Mortgage Obligations (CMOs)—that pass payments through from a class of assets, such as residential mortgages, often with enhanced yields, to comparably rated securities. These are terms to remember for investments that were "too good to be true" but were often marketed as extremely safe. In many cases, they were insured and guaranteed to enhance their creditworthiness as sound investments. In 2006, the subprime-mortgage-backed CDOs/CMOs became a causal element in the mortgage crisis and collapse of the housing market in the U.S. In 2007, the housing bubble finally burst because the underlying assets proved to be worth far less than advertised, forcing many insurers and guarantors to file for bankruptcy. CDOs became one of the best examples ever of investors being taught (sold) what to think instead of how to think. Stories now exist around the world about individual retail investors who lost much of what they had saved for their entire lives on an investment in a "collateralized debt obligation CDO" that they never fully understood, where "collateral" and "obligation" were at best exaggerated or at worst never actually existed. Hopefully the "Next Generation" will remember that if it's about "your money" and it seems too good to be true ... it is. As Warren Buffet predicted, CDOs were the "financial weapons of mass destruction."

mortgage backed securities, <u>CDOs</u> and other "structured products," as they like to call them. Then, as we saw in the mortgage crisis, they give them bogus ratings to ensure their non-existent high quality and safety. Keep thinking ... Is the cash even safe when all they need to do to make it worth less is print more?)

100 trillion dollar bill from Zimbabwe – would currently buy about three eggs.

Inflation

Generally considered to be a rise in the aggregate level of prices. There is common agreement that one cause of high inflation is printing money or, put another way, the unreasonable increase in the money supply. The currency above is from Zimbabwe, where inflation was 7% in 1980. In less than 30 years, Zimbabwe's inflation had risen to 231,000,000%. Yes, acccording to Wikipedia, that is an official number as of July 2008.

Answering the question "Why should you invest in it?" helps you make a better decision about "What type of real estate investment?" Are you interested in investing just money, just time, or both? Do you want to be an investor or a landlord? Next, examine the field of possible real estate investments that you may want to rule out for now and some of the reasons why.

For example, buying lots or bare land can often be done with less capital than "built" real estate, or working farms or forests. Its big drawback, of course, is that by definition it produces no income other than increase in value that isn't realized until sale or development. And it has costs in addition to the purchase

Profit

For our purposes here, profit is what you are hoping to gain on a sale over what you paid to acquire a given investment. The point about profit is that it is a much more difficult calculation to arrive at for fixed assets as compared to liquid assets because of differing laws, tax considerations, and methods available for valuations ... just to name a few. There are, however, advantages to investments in fixed assets (like small income-producing properties) that can make it more than worth the difficulty. You might want to think of these advantages as invisible income or benefits to owning. Liquid assets have the advantage of just that ... being liquid (i.e., easily convertible to cash). Fixed assets have all the advantages we've discussed in this book, such as depreciation, which may be a source of cash. We suggest you take all the advantages of both and manage your profit.

price or mortgage in taxes, maintenance and protection. Even bare land needs to be maintained to retain its value since if any vegetation at all is present, it may need mowing, and will need fire protection and protection from encroachment by refuse dumpers or trespassers. One classical recipe for buying potential development land is to go to a growing town, go out of town until land starts to sell by the acre rather than by the lot, and buy judiciously. Buying judiciously is, of course, the key. In addition to the usual "location, location, location" advice, buying well means a clear title, and knowing the exact legal boundaries. It also requires knowing what is happening on neighboring land. Unoccupied land tends to attract negative attention from neighbors, so you must keep an eye on your property. As the saying has it, "people don't do what is expected, they do what is inspected." But bare land bought at a good price (pay very close attention to comparable sales and trends in the immediate neighborhood) has brought a nice <u>profit</u> to many beginning investors who could not afford "built" property. Just remember that it is more speculative, since the "higher and better use" has not actually been realized, as in an existing building or developed area.

§

The first property I (Glen) was involved in buying wasn't purchased as an investment, but it did have a gravel pit that could have been a source of income. We had bought 30 acres in Maine, and part of the deal was that the seller be allowed to have access and use rock from that gravel pit to build a road across Big Indian Pond to Birch Island, a small island in the middle of the lake. In return for the access and gravel, we received (remember "first right of refusal") a chance to buy a lot on the island for a really good price when the road was done. Even better, we were to be one of the first in line to choose the lot we wanted. At $3,500 with $350 down, it was a good price even then for a lakefront lot on an island with its own private road. You can buy land as an investment, but for our purposes it should eventually produce income. Let's look at a couple of options for income-producing investments you may or may not find suitable and why.

Farms and Forests

Farms and working forests can and usually do have an income stream attached to them, so let's consider them for a minute. Farming is a complex and highly technical occupation and financial pursuit. Do you know what soybean futures are? Do you know what to do about cattle grubs? Have you ever thought about how much fences cost and how hard they are to install and maintain? Do you get high from trying to outguess the weather, having bet a lot of money on it? Farming and owning farmland can be both personally and financially rewarding, but the "premium to knowledge" in farming is enormous, and the supply of really good farmland and really good farmers is quite restricted. Never buy a farm to operate yourself unless it contains mostly the former (good land) and you are one of the latter (a good farmer). We also suggest you don't buy a farm for other people to operate unless you know a great deal about farming in that specific location. Yes, you can have a house with a few acres, and even a cow and a dog, but that is a house, not a farm.

Owning forestland is quite different from owning farmland. For one thing, most farms have at least the possibility of an annual positive cash flow. Unless you can afford quite a lot of forestland, that is unlikely to be so for a forest property. Harvests are often years apart, and wood harvests are usually the major form of income from a forest. Thus, you must be able to carry management costs, taxes, insurance, and all other costs between widely spaced income events. Also, just like farming, modern forest management is a highly technical, knowledge-based enterprise. Do you know what basal area is? How about emerald ash borers? Can you do a statistically sound inventory of a forest property? Could you even find the boundaries of one? How do you feel about snakes and mosquitoes?

Regardless of your answers to these questions, here are a few things to consider before buying a forest:

1. As with any other investment, what you pay for forestland is the major determinant of its later value. And like mutual funds,

the expenses associated with the investment process are major determinants of financial performance.

It is easy to pay too much for forestland. The small, well-located (with respect to roads and markets) parcels usually owned by retail investors are at or near all-time high prices in most areas. But it is still preferable to own your own land directly, without an intermediary, the attendant fees, or the risks of mismanagement. This is similar to direct investment in rental property. Ownership confers control. Of course, along with that control comes a whole suite of responsibilities, from paying taxes to fire protection.

2. Almost every forest property (though initially purchased to produce income from timber sales or perhaps ecosystem services, such as carbon or recreation) has some potential as "real estate" for housing or commercial development. On remote properties, this may be a remote possibility, but fortunes have been made converting forests to house and business lots. This "higher and better use" (HBU) potential should be evaluated carefully for every forest property you consider buying. Again, this is similar to rental real estate in that location is a key to current and future value. Forest appraisal is used to estimate forest value, but it's an excruciating blend of art, science and guesswork. Truly comparable sales are often scarce; future timber prices are hard to predict; and see HBU above. Unless you are completely satisfied with the inventory and location, stay far away from a potential investment, regardless of the appraised price.

3. Forestry is a long-term business, so look carefully at estimates of long-term timber and land price appreciation versus your investment period (often fairly short term). For example, in

2009 we saw lumber prices approximately halved in the Pacific Northwest. "Leveraged" forestland (purchased with a large debt component) often forces owners to sell in a down market to service the debt, meaning that you end up "averaging down" on timber prices for the life of the investment. Thus, the analogy with the stock market seems to hold with forestland: fairly high returns are possible over the long term. In the long term, however, we are all dead. Be very realistic about how long you will own the land. The grandchild test isn't a bad one: Can you envision the investment period lasting until your grandchildren are your age? Even intensive culture forests are relatively slow to produce returns in comparison with a human life span. Major changes in industrial forestland ownership seem mostly to be over, at least in the sense of the large, vertically integrated companies selling off their land. REITs (Real Estate Investment Trusts, such as Plumb Creek and Rayonier), TIMOs (Timber Investment Management Organizations, such as Hancock and Forestland Group) are currently major owners, but for how long? How will the market be when you want to sell? Will they be selling too? Forest investments make money and lose money just like other investments. The returns reported for the TIMOS (above) have fallen steadily for a decade.

4. Once you have bought forestland, managing it as an investment begins. Bookends for styles of forest management are 1) very intensive management (high capital investment, high and relatively fast gross returns) or 2) very extensive management (just cut trees, relying on natural regeneration). The latter provides lower, and often slower, gross returns but also much lower investment and carrying costs, which can reward extensive management with higher net returns than the intensive kind.

All gradations of management intensity are observable and available to investors. The key here is to avoid the "fallacy of the middle": relatively high initial investment, modest growth, a long time to carry upfront costs, and concomitant low returns.

Plantations, for example, tend to have a high initial cost and faster growth. With more invested early, more is at risk in the long run than with naturally regenerated forests; however, returns per unit time and area can be much higher than with natural forests, particularly if the plantations produce a high value added product (veneer, for example).

For natural forests, it is imperative to know merchantable timber volume (now and in the future), ease of regeneration, and particularly, "regulatory risk." Basically, regulatory risk means that some governmental body or social convention might keep you from cutting and selling your trees when it is time to do so. Sustained yield and certification schemes can work for the investor to reduce market and regulatory risk. Buying the right forestland at a reasonable price and engaging competent managers with deep, local knowledge of forests, regulations, and markets is the right formula.

In summary, if you think you might want to invest in forestland, consider these points:

Make forest investments fit your own specific time and lifestyle goals, and fit them into your investment portfolio or overall picture. It is easy to fall in love with a piece of forestland. When that happens, make sure your head, as well as your heart, is engaged in the evaluation process. There is nothing wrong with owning forestland simply because you like it. Just don't confuse that with making money.

Pooled funds versus direct ownership. Pooled funds have experts who buy the land, but they buy it with cash in their pocket (moral hazard). Direct ownership requires more work but provides more control and higher returns with lower fees (if you're willing to do the work).

REITs, TIMOs, and limited partnerships are forestland vehicles that can work, but pay careful attention to management fees and the role of the managing partner. Know what was paid for the forestland when acquired versus market rates when you buy in. Know the time horizon for real gain.

Invest where valuable trees grow readily, not necessarily rapidly, since competition with brush and weeds often limits regeneration and growth where trees grow most rapidly.

Invest in accessible land (good existing roads) with high site index value (good soils and microclimate).

Assess natural risks before buying: insects, disease, fire, ice, wind, etc.

Assess political risks before buying: environmental and transportation regulations, political attitudes toward the timber business, etc.

Initial price and condition are the key to future gains or losses, but good price and condition alone do not guarantee success. Management, politics, markets and larger world forces such as demographics and wars profoundly affect all forests directly or indirectly. As with a rental property, when you buy a forest, you are buying a piece of the society around it as well.

Above all, learn everything you can. Get the best impartial advice, and look for a premium to knowledge. **Forests are the least understood major asset category.**

The take home lesson here is that forests and farms are an order of magnitude harder than small rental properties as a beginning real estate investment. So for all the reasons above, unless you have special knowledge and experience, don't jump into forestry or farming. But if you have the money to do it at an economical scale, and the will to acquire the expertise, farms and forests can be satisfying and lucrative investments.

Residential Income Properties

We believe the best long-term opportunity exists in small, residential income properties in good locations. These properties are more likely in your comfort zone because they would be similar to what you are used to living in. That means for now we are ruling out commercial property and large apartment complexes. Commercial property may be headed for its own crisis in the years to come. Overbuilt and over-leveraged, it is now under-performing, and may soon be headed for a substantial loss in value depending on location. Larger apartment complexes can be ruled out for now as well because we are assuming you don't have any substantial experience. Again, remember the saying:

> "Good judgment comes from experience,
> and experience comes from bad judgment."

At this point, when you're considering income properties as part of your allocation of investments, keep your mistakes small. Remember, any strategy might have worked in an appreciating market, but it won't work anymore.

Much of the reason for investing in smaller residential income properties has to do with the economies of scale. When you are beginning to invest in any kind of income property, bigger is not always better. It's not only possible, but likely, that you already own a home. When you're getting started, you will probably be the property manager, the maintenance person, the accountant, and the person going to court when things go wrong just like at your own home. This is a good time to be cautious and pick an investment that you are at least somewhat familiar with. A good first choice would be a small property that has demand and income but is manageable considering the skills and time suitable for your personal situation.

In order to make our arguments relevant to the greatest number of people with the greatest need to make a serious change in the way they are likely to invest, we need to make assumptions about you. We assume you are headed to a retirement disaster, about to jump from the frying pan of being the "Next Generation" frustrated by financial uncertainty into the fire of making the wrong investment choices. We also assume you have already thought about investing in residential properties, and even think it could be a really good fit for you. It is reasonable, then, to expect to be faced with a very steep learning curve (under the best of circumstances). Our purpose here is to make that learning curve a bit less steep, measurably safer, and to give you a softer landing from the parts where you may fall off. So if commercial real estate, large apartment complexes and land in general are ruled out for now, the question is what is left and why?

What is left are the small residential properties that we think offer the best long-term results, ranging from single-family houses to small apartment buildings (eight units or less) in great locations.

Every real estate book you ever read will most likely emphasize location. It's true, but what does that mean? Well, a great location means the difference between success and failure for your investment and your work. A great location should mean at least two things to you. First, that there are demographic drivers that will make your location a success. Second, that there are unique advantages or what we call "potential" that will make this particular property a success.

A good example of a demographic driver would be students in a college town. The demand for your units is enhanced by the fact that the students need a place to rent while in school and want it close to the college. Let's imagine you own a four-plex next to campus. You'll likely have a higher turnover, but in return you will have a long-term, built-in stream of tenants competing to rent your property. A good example of "potential" would be things like: closer proximity to the university, extra land that could be built on in the future, or even unused space that could be converted into rentable space. We had a property with a very large porch that we later converted easily into an additional apartment.

What we'll argue repeatedly is the need for demand. Without demand your property is worthless, maybe even worse than worthless. Worthless just means "zero value." As we have seen in this recession, property can sometimes have a negative value where you owe more than the property is worth, commonly referred to as being "upside down" in your property. You must have demand for your property in order for your investment to be successful, to appreciate, and for you not to become upside down.

To a large extent, location determines demand. Your knowledge of a location and the demographic drivers of that area are your competitive advantage. We were both university teachers, so we know universities and we know students. Our investments are usually close to universities. What will be your competitive advantage? You may know hospitals, industries, ethnic populations, or even geographic areas like suburbs.

We may go so far as to agree on the best type of real estate investment and the reasons for investing in it. But only you can decide on the actual property and the specific location. Demand for your property will make your decision to jump out of that frying pan a good idea, and lack of demand will burn you in the fire. Don't underestimate the benefits of demand. Buy good property in a good location.

You can manage demand, but you can't really create it. There is a point of diminishing returns where your cash flow becomes so negative it won't allow for any more adjustment and you won't be able to meet your obligations on the property. Don't put yourself in this situation, *ever*. If you don't know who is going to rent your apartments, it probably won't be anyone you're going to like.

What real estate investment should you choose to start with? The obvious answer is small residential income properties with strong demographic drivers that are easy to rent (easier than the other similar properties) to qualified tenants and make financial sense. We will explain what we mean by financial sense in the next chapter, but there is no financial sense without demand, which only comes with a good property in a great location.

We urge you to think about the time value of money and start now. Find your competitive edge, find your location, and start looking for deals. Waiting is not a good strategy!

John's family has a story that is pertinent here. It seems that in the 19th century, Uncle Elmore liked to sit in the "hot stove league" at the general store and tell stories of his pioneer past in southern Indiana.

He used to say, "You know, boys, when I came here all these creeks were full of gold nuggets."

The other stove focus group participants thought about this for a while. Finally, one of them said, "But Elmore, you don't have any money. Why didn't you pick up some of that gold when you had the chance?"

Uncle Elmore looked surprised and said, "Well, you know, boys, I just didn't have the time!"

Don't be Uncle Elmore. Get going. Now.

"Don't wait to buy real estate. Buy real estate and wait."

ROBERT G. ALLEN

4

When Buying Investment Real Estate, Be Positive But Very Selective

Location, Remember, Location

IT'S VERY IMPORTANT that you understand this chapter, so pay close attention. Chapter 4 explains how to develop a successful analysis of residential income property, which in turn will guide you into the ownership of successful real estate investments. **Section 1** explains why you need it. **Section 2** explains how you do it and some of what not to do as you try. **Section 3** includes case studies with analysis, outcomes and comparisons of example properties for your review. What you do after that is up to you.

Section 1

When we recommend buying investment real estate, and being positive but very selective, most people ask us how. It is not at all uncommon to find yourself saying, "I found a property I like. Should I buy it? How do I figure this out?" This is a question even experienced investors struggle with. "How much should I pay, and under what terms?" The reason for the struggle is that the answer is almost always the same no matter who you ask. The answer? Sure, buy it. But only if it's a good deal. What does that even mean? How do you know if it is? Life is full of *ifs*. You need to make this *if* a *when*.

A Tale of Luck, Value and a Goal

Back to that story about the 30 acres. My parents (Glen's) never owned a home, or any real estate for that matter. They did, however, tell me about all the ones they would have, should have and could have bought, and regretted that they didn't. One of their favorite Sunday afternoon activities was to go on a drive and point out all the homes they should have bought. Needless to say, as a child this was one of my least favorite activities for a Sunday afternoon. But something in those Sunday drives stuck in my mind.

When I was a student at NYU living in a fourth floor walk-up, I used to read catalogues of farm property for sale in Maine, where land was still very inexpensive. The catalogues had everything from large farms and timberlands to small parcels of just a few acres. The prices seemed so reasonable compared to New York City. But how could I know if it would appreciate? I didn't, not a clue. There was no analysis. It was just a cash deal with no income to consider. The value on this deal was in the doing. Personal value, not financial value. Because of that, there was no risk. We only bought what we could afford, and it didn't matter if it went up, down or stayed the same for the rest of my life. I had accomplished something I had long wanted to: I owned 30 acres in Maine!

There can be value in having a goal, a plan, and in closing the deal on your plan. The value at that moment was probably only visible to me. No one else could see it then, but they can see it clearly now. I had gotten to do something my parents had only dreamed about.

The deed said "30 acres more or less," but I know I got a lot more. Was it smart? Lucky? A bit of both? Sure, but most importantly, as I look back now after 40 years, I think the significance of this is doing something that would eventually lead to doing more.

§

Now for the big question: Are you going to do anything? Are you going to do something that leads to doing more? Oh, we can hear your objections from here, but we can deal with those in a while. For now, let's keep thinking about this idea of financial independence and remember there was no income on that land in Maine. You may start with an investment in land, too, just to get started, but what you really want is income property. For success with that, you must know how to correctly calculate the cost, income and expenses on an income property investment.

Buying income property that you *own and control* is a critical asset class you should seriously consider as part of your investment plan. It's also a key step toward a well-balanced, diversified financial plan for you, the Next Generation, to reach financial independence.

The Income Property Analysis in this chapter is your road map. It's clearly marked with signs telling you when to keep trying, when to stop, and even when to get out. It will help you answer that question of *if* (but only *help*). It helps because it makes you think! It helps you see the exit signs and warns you when to slow down. It helps you think by giving you a comparable range of prices that you would be interested in and agreeable to paying for a given property. This range of prices— the difference between what you would *realistically* like to pay and your *real* final offer when you're ready to walk away—is what we call offering price elasticity. This gives you a range of offering prices you can work with, but it will only be accurate if you have also correctly identified and incorporated the qualitative parameters of the property and a serious self-evaluation of your personal circumstances.

Offering Price Elasticity

The amount of wiggle room or variance you have between the seller's offering price and what they will actually take for the property. This elasticity also includes the variance in the terms and time as components of the price. Use them all wisely.

The analysis of a residential income property investment you are considering, or will be considering sometime in the future, is a tool. The way we use this tool, and hope will be helpful to you, is to point out areas of both serious financial concern and potential investment opportunity. Like any tool (and this is just one of your tools), it has to be used correctly. As the saying goes, "If your only tool is a hammer, then every problem is a nail." This tool gets you past some serious *ifs*. The final decision, however, on a residential income property investment should always be based on more than just price elasticity and quantitative information.

Property analysis cannot be replaced by general rules of thumb or heuristics, like "never pay full price" or "rent your property monthly for 1% of the purchase price." These rules of thumb can be helpful but may also be misleading. Maybe the property is worth the full price! I have lost more money over-bargaining on properties than I care to think about. Maybe you won't get 1% a month because you're paying a premium for a great location. There are plenty of properties in Detroit right now you can get for less than asking price. "If" you could rent them, you would do better than 1% a month.

There are two financial parts of your investment—the price and the terms—both of which are specific to you and this particular property, and both need to be reviewed and analyzed carefully.

As you work through this analysis, you will have the opportunity to blend your financial decision-making and investment restrictions into a better understanding of a given property. The property analysis becomes a "planning tool." When you conclude an analysis like this, you will have incorporated quantitative financial assumptions and projections with qualitative lifestyle and risk-factor issues critically important to your personal situation for a specific income property investment opportunity.

Once you begin to blend quantitative premises—income, vacancy rates, expenses, loan-to-value requirements—with your own qualitative opinions about personal preferences—location, zoning, property condition, the time required to manage this type of investment—you will be in a position to weigh your alternatives. These alternatives will affect every number you use in your analysis. For example, if you push the rents, it may result in higher vacancy or turnover. If you cut your repair and maintenance budget, it may impair your rental income. In the analysis, you have the chance to balance what you think you can do with the price/debt/equity/income/expenses, and simulate how

Loan-To-Value Ratio

Another common ratio used to determine your equity or risk capital invested in a property. Don't be surprised if you need as much as 25%–30% down on property that is being used for investment purposes. Often any property under four units isn't considered commercial property and may qualify for a better interest rate or lower down payment, so don't hesitate to shop for these rates.

Vacancy Rate

A good measure of how you are treating your tenants and managing your property. If you don't think your tenants are your partners in the success of this venture, see how you feel when it's empty for a while.

that will affect you both short and long term under the assumptions you have made.

So the analysis comes into play when there is a financial opportunity involving residential income property we would like to explore by simulating the effects of financial outcomes based on differing financial premises. Doing this allows us to look forward and see the consequences of our choices without any real risk of financial harm.

Financial choices aside, what we really have to be concerned with, as our life leadership line in Chapter 2 showed us, is that hesitation can become procrastination, and procrastination can become regret. As we look back on our lives, which do you think we will regret more: those things we might have done, and done well, but never did for fear of failing, or the things we tried to do but failed, and then had to try again in order to succeed?

We challenge you at this point to explain what failure means to you in the context of this discussion.

Be specific. Use a realistic small income property investment you could make. We're not only talking about the purchase price but also what you could swing as a down payment. Use the analysis and see what assumptions it would require in the world as we know it to make this venture a failure. Since most of us will someday buy a house of our own, let's examine what happens if you buy one as a rental. This would be about the smallest income property investment you can make. Pick any house in an area you think will prosper and grow over the next 30 years; choose any financing currently offered; make the rental income on the low side and the expenses on the high side; and keep the growth in market value (appreciation) low. Be pessimistic. Make it poor and then make it worse. We think you'll very surprised at the effort and level of pessimism it will take to make your investment a failure. Look at it over 5 to 6 years and then again at 25 to 30 years.

Our point being that it's better to have tried and failed than never to have tried at all. Most of us won't be planning to fail. What we *will* do is fail to plan, or even worse, fail to act.

What we would like to do here is point out the real possibilities for success and the stumbling blocks of difficult problems and financial mistakes to avoid as you analyze an investment opportunity in residential income property. As you examine the following, assume you have overcome your hesitation and are looking at financial information that you'll be asked to determine and agree on for your analysis. Remember: Everything here is being critically questioned only to save your assets!

Net Operating Income (NOI)

The income on your property after vacancy, losses and expenses. Before you buy the property, this is just a projection; after the purchase is closed, it becomes an expectation. We recommend you carefully revisit NOI when estimating your underlying expectations about income and expenses. Do this before you buy any income property.

Cash On Cash Return

The annual ratio between the Net Operating Income (NOI) less the debt service and the cash invested in the property:

NOI – DEBT SERVICE / INVESTED CASH = CASH ON CASH RETURN

Don't be surprised if there is little to no cash on cash return. When you're starting, it's not likely you're going to be hitting home runs—try for singles and get on base. Be very careful with debt, but don't be surprised if you have to feed the property. Just make sure it easily fits into your budget, and look at the negative cash flow as a forced savings plan, or dollar cost averaging with real estate that is being used to buy an annuity (see Annuity). In fact, one competitive advantage you may have starting out is your willingness to look at properties that need work and have small negative cash flows that can be fixed and made positive.

Capitalization Rate

The ratio of Net Operating Income (NOI) to what you are paying for the property:

NOI / PURCHASE PRICE

This is a market-driven number, so you have two problems with it. First, is it competitive with the going rate for similar properties in the area? Second, is it accurate?

The following elements need to be addressed in order to complete the Income Property Analysis:

What You Need To Know	What You Were Told	What You Confirmed
NAME OF BUILDING		
ADDRESS OF BUILDING		
TOTAL UNITS		
PROJECTED MONTHLY RENT PER UNIT		
OTHER ANNUAL INCOME		
SCHEDULED GROSS INCOME		
MARKET PRICE		
IMPROVEMENTS		
LAND		
SALVAGE VALUE		
MARKET PRICE PER UNIT		
SQUARE FOOTAGE		
DEPRECIATION METHOD		
EXISTING LOANS: AMOUNT, INTEREST RATE, N (LIFE OF THE LOAN), PAYMENTS		
VACANCY AND CREDIT LOSSES		
GROSS OPERATING INCOME		
OPERATING EXPENSE: ALL OF WHICH WILL BE DISCUSSED IN DETAIL		
TOTAL OPERATING INCOME		
CAPITALIZATION RATE: "THE MEASURE OF YOUR RETURN"		

Since income property is generally valued using projected cap rates, you need to make sure the numbers you're using (or someone else has given you) to calculate NOI are accurate. Income can be exaggerated and expenses can be understated, which will make your cap rate meaningless. Cap rates are also market driven so you need cap rates from comparable properties.

We've been given exaggerated cap rates many times with misleading sales information. One example was on an 18-unit apartment building. It had a good cap rate and, upon further examination, we found out why: It had total repair expenses listed at $1,000 for the entire previous year. It should have been more than that per unit. No matter if this was purposely misrepresented or the seller was doing a really poor job keeping up the property, it would have been a bad deal for us. We have also seen properties with good cap rates and high rents, where the seller had given generous incentives to the tenants in order to raise the rents and make the cap rate appear to be better than it really was. Be careful not to accept a cap rate to make your investment decision unless you check it carefully. Your job is to find an investment where the cap rate is reasonable but rents are low, which means the price is probably good even considering the low rents. Buy the property, raise the net income, and thus improve the cap rate. When the cap rate goes up, the value of your investment goes up.

Confirmation is the Essence of Practical Leadership

I (John) have been credited with the saying, "People don't do what is expected, they do what is inspected." I am sure I heard it somewhere else first and didn't originate it. But just as in science, rigorous data checking is at the heart of investing, and perhaps particularly real estate investing. As President Reagan tried to say in Russian, "Trust, but verify." Check your facts, and check the checking. Be pessimistic, just for the purposes of this exercise. One of the great forestland managers and forest economists of his generation, John Beuter, put it this way: "Your arguments are not to convince your pal beside you in the pickup. They have to be good enough for an angry Harvard lawyer who doesn't like you." Pretend you are that Harvard lawyer when you evaluate a possible purchase. Take adverse advice. Let reality leak in. As a treasured mentor once said, "Science is what you can prove wrong if it is wrong. Philosophy is what you can only argue about." Keep philosophy, in this sense, away from your real estate decisions.

Section 2

Before you make a binding decision on a real estate investment, assume that almost everything you have been told by the seller or their agent is completely false, purposefully misleading, wildly optimistic and painfully inaccurate (see above)! Take a look at the following analysis and examine each element/assumption for error and opportunity.

Realtors and real estate professionals can provide valuable services and are usually honest and knowledgeable; however, they often represent the seller *and* the seller's best interest. First, question all the assumptions you'll be relying on to reach your conclusion and decision. Remember that this analysis is only for the financial functionality of your investment. It does not address the legal, personal or practical aspects of making a sound residential real estate investment! You need to carefully examine this too. You say you did? Good. Now let's look at our investment plan. Did we mention location?

The Offer

So often everyone wants to analyze everything before they have anything. I (Glen) do something similar when I go fishing and plan the big dinner around what I'm going to catch before I catch a thing. Not the best idea! Remember: At this stage, you don't have anything to analyze! You need to make an offer first.

This whole process of making an offer is a mine field for most of us. We want to make a good offer to avoid losing a property we really think would work. We also don't want to be locked into something we can't get out of and overpay for the property. Keep in mind these are optimistic folks who put that price on their property. It's entirely possible what they're asking is completely out of line with reality and only something they are hoping for. But if you lowball the offer, you risk losing the property. Do you care? Would you rather own a property right now knowing you paid too much or wait for a property that makes sense for you? The seller and the seller's agent will be long gone and you alone will have the responsibility to make this work.

And ... their agent gets paid how much? Says who? Where is it written? Right ... totally open to negotiation, just like the price. The price is what they would like to get. That commission is what they would like to get. The part I really like is when they tell you the seller is paying the commission! Right ... then why are you the only one putting any money in?

Be patient and make the offer that you think works for you. Remember: You are the only one who will be responsible for the future success of the property. At this point you are just fishing. What you're fishing for is information. You want to know the price and terms acceptable to the seller so you can begin your inspections and analyze your offer with real numbers. It's very common for negotiations on a property to go on over extended periods of time with lots of back-and-forth offers and counter offers. Sometimes, however, the process is quick. Everyone agrees and moves forward to a closing right away. Here is a story of the opposite.

A Tale of Interest and Time

The first time we saw this five-plex for sale in the early 1980s it was listed at $225,000. We made a full price offer contingent on the seller carrying the contract with $25,000 down. At the time, interest rates were very high. Twelve percent was common and we all agreed on it. The deal fell apart because the seller wanted their money over five years, which would have made the cash flow on this property impossible for us to manage. We really liked this five-plex, and the great location, so we made at least five offers over the next three years. All the offers fell through because of the seller's demand for a short contract. Also, our offers were getting lower because the economy was bad, the real estate market was worse, and the property was being neglected. Each time we would let it sit and try again with the same result.

Then I got a call out of the blue from the seller asking me what I thought they should sell it for. Wow! I said I would ask my partner and get back to them. We said we would offer $70,000 cash. Guess what. They said they had to have $74,000. We said forget it. Two months later we saw it in the paper advertised for $65,000. I called the realtor, offered $60,000 cash, and they took it. So they took a big loss, right? They could have sold it for $225,000, but they waited too long, got greedy, missed the market, and sold it for $60,000. That's a loss of $165,000, right? Not really, not the only loss.

Remember the $225,000 offer and 12% interest on the balance of $200,000 for 30 years they rejected? They would have made more in interest on the contract for the property in three years than they got in total for the property by the time it finally sold and closed. Just think if they had sold it for $225,000 with a large pre-payment penalty to us and made it hard to pay off early. We would just now be paying it off. We would have paid $225,000 for the property and over $540,000 in interest over the 30 years.

To put even more emphasis on this point, imagine if that interest they lost by refusing the contract had been reinvested. The monthly payment to them would have been about $2,057 for 30 years. If they had invested the $25,000 they received from us as a down payment and invested just half of our monthly payment (about $1,000) for those 30 years at 7%, which was possible, they would have made over an additional $1,300,000. So, let's see … They lost the difference in the sale price of $165,000. They lost $540,000 in potential interest income. And they lost over $1,300,000 in the probable opportunity costs of not having that income to invest. That makes for a rough (pun intended) total loss of over $2,000,000.

§

Lucky for us you can make counter offers. I'm sure you can question our assumptions on reaching that total, but no matter how you look at this, it was really a series of poor financial decisions by the seller. Would the sellers do this differently now? Probably. Were they wrong to sell? Probably not, just tired and not wanting to manage the property any longer. We all understand that hindsight isn't foresight and that we all have 20/20 vision looking back. Hopefully, you'll now have the benefit of foresight from this story, and see the time value of money and that a deal always has at least two parts—price and terms.

If you are to build a future for yourself, you have to look forward, even when there's risk and work. So if investing in income property is your goal, don't worry. Make the offer. All they can do is say no, and maybe not invite you to their birthday party. **You don't have to do any analysis to make an offer, but you better do a very careful analysis before you make a final agreement to purchase a property.** Make the offer contingent on every single thing you're worried about, but make the offer and get the property <u>under contract</u>.

Under Contract

This term means different things in different places and to different people. Usually it means there is an accepted offer in good faith by a willing seller and a willing buyer with contingencies still to work out, but it doesn't mean the deal is done. At best it means there is an ongoing negotiation that technically continues right up to the moment it closes. It could mean the seller accepted an offer an hour ago or that the deal has been smoothly progressing and will close today. The point being that if you are really interested in a particular property and have been told it's under contract, don't hesitate to ask for details and express interest in improving the offer. Just be sure to leave your contact information. It's not at all unusual for a deal that's under contract to fall through and go to the next in line. A word of caution to the buyer: Don't get bullied during negotiations once you're under contract, but don't over-negotiate and lose a property you might have been smart to own.

Under contract means the buyer and the seller have agreed on the basic terms and price and will begin to negotiate based on the outcome of all the contingencies. These contingencies, just to list a few, might be your analysis, financing, condition, pest and dry rot, accountant's and attorney's approval, partner's approval, and did we say completion of your analysis, the results of which are subject to your approval. Every property will likely have different contingencies. Make sure you list yours carefully. Check and double-check everything! This is your way out when you see a red flag and it becomes more than just a red flag. Be sure you have a way out and make the offer. Once it's accepted, you can work on your numbers because now you have the numbers to work on. You have a binding offer to sell from the seller and a chance to really look things over before you make a final decision. Hey! What about my earnest money? I don't want to lose that. We don't blame you. Don't give them any, or if you do, make sure you can get it back if you don't want the property! Don't hesitate to use your attorney and accountant to help you with this step. If possible, give the seller a note and make the note part of the earnest money agreement—**the one you have a way out of, right?** Did we mention location? Did we mention check everything? Remember: The problems and opportunities are in the details.

A Tale of Verification

One of us (John) wanted to move to a new house on a lake where he was working in Wisconsin—beautiful lake, clear, full of fish, great views, 200 feet of lakeshore. Fortunately, we made the offer contingent on proof of lakeshore ownership by the seller. We were told this was obstructionist and probably un-American. How could they not own the lakeshore when theirs was the only house between the land and the lake? Yada yada yada ... We insisted. The original deed, in fact, left a band of land between the house lot and the lake. The seller had to get a quit claim deed from the heirs of a defunct timber company to convey clear title to the lakeshore.

§

Number of Units, Bedrooms and Bathrooms

It's hard to believe that what you think you're buying might not be what you're buying, right? But, yes, it may not be. Look carefully. It could be better or it could be worse. Again, check and double-check. We once made an offer on two duplexes and on inspection found eight extra bedrooms, two extra bathrooms and even two laundry rooms that were not included in the sales material. It was listed as two, two-bedroom one-bath duplexes but turned out to be two four-bedroom two-bath duplexes with laundry rooms. The price was so-so for what it was advertised as but fantastic for what it turned out to be.

The owner knew what it was but no one else did because it was advertised incorrectly. He wasn't getting any "lookers" and accepted our offer. There are probably more stories where investors got *less* than they thought they were getting. Look carefully. Could be good, could be bad. Did we mention that you should check and double-check?

Projected Monthly Rent

Be very careful here. It's not uncommon for the seller to give you projections of what they would like their rents to be instead of what they actually are. Rental income often gets exaggerated or manipulated to inflate the value of the property. Common ways to do this include: 1) Giving you rent projections that represent what they would like to have, instead of the actual historical rents; 2) Ignoring the fact that one of their units is occupied by a resident manager who pays no rent; 3) Guaranteeing rents for a few years after the purchase (remember you're buying it long term and will probably have the property after these guarantees are gone); 4) Giving away free rent to tenants who sign leases at a rate higher than market in anticipation of selling the property (e.g., "Two months free rent with a one-year lease"). All you see are the higher rents. The tenants actually pay lowered rents, the owner/seller receives less income over the term of the lease, and you paid extra for the property thinking you would always be getting those great rents. Don't do it! Study the leases and make the seller show you their tax returns for the last three years. There are many ways to mislead a buyer. Don't let anyone mislead you.

On the other side of this pancake it's not at all uncommon for rents to be understated. There is always the chance that the seller is an incompetent manager or maybe one that's just worn out. Perhaps the seller has not kept their rents up with the going market rate as their investment and their attitude slipped into disrepair. Often, if the building is a bit run down, the rents will be low for the market. Here you have an opportunity to easily upgrade the property and raise the rents, which could be a big factor in helping you decide on this investment. Future income is what determines the future value of your residential income property.

A Tale of the House Next Door

The first income property I (Glen) was involved with was the house next door, literally. My neighbor and I had talked and he told me he would let me know whenever he was ready to sell. My problem was that I was in graduate school and had about $500 total in savings and two kids. When the time came to sell, he wanted $23,000. It was a good price and great location only half a block to the university. It was in absolutely awful shape! The upstairs was a rooming house, and in the downstairs his wife ran a day school. Of course when he goes, so does she and the day school. After looking it over, it seemed we could easily get five more rooms into the downstairs to go with the five upstairs for a total of 10 rentable rooms, two kitchens and two bathrooms. These rooms would easily rent for $50 a month (this was 1973). This would be about double the income the seller was getting on the upstairs, and I would get the downstairs income as well.

Armed with all this information, I visited our local credit union and was told they would make a loan on the property, but only for $19,000 ... a lot less than I needed. After further conversations with my neighbor, he told me he really needed $11,000 cash to buy his retirement ranch in Texas and he could carry a note or second mortgage for the balance if that would help me. It did!

This property also needed lots of work, and that is not an exaggeration! He had only painted the outside as high as he could reach, and it had 18 broken windows (another story). I also had to convert the downstairs into rooms before I would be getting any income.

So here is what I did (with my neighbor's help). I borrowed the $19,000 and gave him $14,000 ($3,000 more than he needed for his ranch). He had wanted $23,000, so I owed the bank $19,000 on the first mortgage and I owed him $9,000 on a second mortgage, for a total of $28,000. Pretty good so far … If I do the deal, I get $5,000 cash, I get the house, I get twice the number of rooms and twice the current rent ($500 a month if I can fill it up).

Of course I had payments to make of $190 a month plus taxes, insurance and all the upkeep. Ouch! Looking at it now, it seems like a no-brainer. Back then, with $500 in the bank, it was very scary and I was very worried. But I had my analysis, exactly like the one you're working with now (but done in pencil … remember it was 1973).

I was also taking Finance in my MBA program and went to talk with my professor about what to do. "What to do?" He looked it over, gave a nice smile and asked, "Why would anyone ever do something like this?" The work, the rundown condition, 10 rooms that need to be remodeled and rented out … definitely not for him. But he did say he thought the location was great and my long-term analysis was correct (i.e., he believed I would make money on it).

That convinced me. I did the deal and I'm glad I did. Still have the house, still half a block from campus, still trouble now and then. But it's all paid off and the rooms rent for about 10 times what they originally did. Oh, and it's now worth a lot more than I paid for it. This investment was made a long time ago, but the ideas in these stories are still current and valid. The only thing that's changed are the prices. Did we mention location?

Other Annual Income

Don't overlook other sources of income. Is there a laundry room? Who owns the machines? That's correct on ours ... we do. We really like it when some of your income is delivered in bags that are too heavy to carry (quarters are heavy)! Just joking, we can carry most of them. You also get great write-offs on the equipment that you now own. How about garages or storage units? Who says they automatically go with the apartments? They don't have to unless it's a selling point for the apartment. Here in a university town I have even seen some folks park cars on their property on game days. Put 100 cars on your property at $20/car and that's "other income." Did we mention location?

Expenses

As we discussed previously, be very cautious of accepting any-one's input on the expenses associated with an income property investment until you have personally confirmed their accuracy. Remember the phrase "garbage in garbage out"?

Section 3

What does it all mean? Where's the beef? Let's start with a case study of a rental house. We will run through the analysis twice—first with optimistic but realistic estimates, then with pessimistic estimates—and see how we do.

For our imaginary case study, let's imagine it's a property you have found and are interested in, but we'll use our numbers for the analysis to demonstrate a point.

You often hear that it's the journey, not the destination, that's important in life. This is especially true with income property investments because of the long-term nature of the journey and the learning curves involved. Remember: No investment means no journey; no journey means no learning curve and no results. Procrastination caused by the fear of life's "what ifs" often stops potential income property investors in their tracks. We mention this here for a reason, a strong reason: Your financial future! Buy property where the results of your efforts are management issues and not economic issues. If the economy where your property is located goes bad, consider cutting your losses and getting out. If it's already bad, don't get in! Buy where you understand the economic drivers of the community you are investing in and feel extremely optimistic about the growth potential for the area. If you don't, don't invest.

We have discussed at length the importance of getting a good price in a good location, without which you may not achieve the results you are forecasting in your analysis. You must have accurate, achievable estimates on everything, especially your income and expenses. Study your assumptions carefully.

Now, looking over the projections for what we guess to be our most likely situation, there are four additional (very important) variables we need to estimate (guess). These are percentage change variables, so we'll make educated guesses and choose wisely.

1. Vacancy rate ...
2. Gross operating income ...
3. Operating expenses ...
4. **Growth in market value** ...

#4 is the big one! If you don't think this is a positive number, don't do this deal!

For our first example/analysis, let's make some conservative estimates. That means if we didn't feel we could reasonably expect this outcome, we wouldn't do this deal. We can live with these estimates and prosper if we achieve no worse:

1. Vacancy … **6%** losses
2. Gross operating income … **4%** annual increases
3. Operating expenses … **3%** annual increases
4. Growth in market value … **5%** appreciation/year

These numbers are estimates and will be "off," but over the long run they are our best guess of what we think we can do. There will be months, maybe even years, when the rent goes down instead of up, expenses are higher, vacancies are higher, and tax laws change. Things change. The building may go down in value instead of up, but long term it's our best guess and this is a long-term investment.

Study the analysis, look at the outcome, and compare it to your life line from Chapter 2. Now look 30 years down the road at both. Add 30 years to your current age, $800,000+ to your net worth, and $20,000+ to your annual income. It can happen … 30 years ago we were writing this analysis on a Sol 20 computer with an IBM electric typewriter for a printer, and using it to buy small apartment buildings.

Pro Forma Property Analysis - Your First Rental House

| Type of Property: | Your First Rental House, with optimistic expectations |
| Location: | Street of your dreams (Is failure worse than regret?) |

	Number of Units	Projected monthly rent / unit
Total Units	1	$1,200
2 Bdrm Units	1	$1,200
1 Bdrm Units	0	$0
Other units	0	$0

Projected annual rental income:	$14,400
Other annual income (Laundry, Fees, etc.):	$0
Scheduled Gross Income	$14,400

Description of Facts

Asking Price:	$215,000	Land:	$50,000
Improvements:	$165,000	Salvage Value:	0
Asking Price / Unit:	$215,000		

Rentable Sq. Footage:	1500

Depreciation Method:	27.5 years	Depreciation / year:	$6,000.00

Proposed Financing

Amount:	$172,000	N =	30
Interest Rate:	6.00%	Annual Payments:	($12,375)
		Monthly Payments:	($1,031)

Part 1 (input) - *Using optimistic but hopefully realistic numbers*

Property Income Statement

Scheduled Gross Income		14,400
(% Vacancy & Credit Losses)	6%	(864)
Gross Operating Income		**13,536**

Less: Operating Expenses

Property Taxes	1,894
Insurance	500
Utilities	-
Licenses / Permits	-
Advertising	-
Management	720
Payroll	-
Supplies	-
Administrative	
Maintenance	1,200
Replacement Reserve	

Total Operating Expenses	**4,314**
Net Operating Income	**9,222**
Capitalization Rate	**0.043**
(Net Operating Income / Market Value)	

Comments:

These examples and calculations are for illustrative purposes only,
and do not reflect actual properties, market values, loans,
operating income or expenses.

Pro Forma Property Analysis - Your First Rental House (results)

	Year 1	Year 5	Year 10
Equity Calculation			
Market Value (Beg)	215,000	261,334	333,536
Less: Total Loans	172,000	162,737	147,559
Owner's Equity	**43,000**	**98,597**	**185,976**
Tax Calculation			
Net Operating Income	9,222	10,980	13,637
Less: Interest	10,263	9,691	8,755
Less: Depreciation	6,000	6,000	6,000
Taxable Income	**(7,041)**	**(4,711)**	**(1,118)**
Income Tax	**(2,464)**	**(1,649)**	**(391)**
Income Tax Rate	0.35	0.35	0.35
Cash Flow Calculation			
Net Operating Income	9,222	10,980	13,637
Less: Financing Pmts	(12,375)	(12,375)	(12,375)
Gross Spendable	**(3,153)**	**(1,395)**	**1,262**
Less: Income Tax	(2,464)	(1,649)	(391)
Net Spendable	**(689)**	**254**	**1,654**
Net Spendable Rate	**(0.016)**	**0.006**	**0.038**
(Net Spendable / Equity)			
Equity Income			
Net Spendable	(689)	254	1,654
Plus: Principal Reduction	2,112	2,684	3,620
Plus: Market Value Growth	-	12,444	15,883
Net Equity Income	**1,424**	**15,382**	**21,156**
Net Equity Income Rate	**0.033**	**0.358**	**0.492**
(Net Equity Income / Equity)			
FYI: Accumulative Market Value Growth	*-*	*46,334*	*118,536*
FYI: Total Interest Paid (accumulative)	*10,263*	*49,927*	*95,687*
FYI: Accumulative Gross Operating Income	*13,536*	*73,315*	*162,515*

Notes on Growth Projections:

*Assumed Gross Operating Income % increase by year =   4%

*Assumed Total Operating Expenses % increase by year =   3%

*Assumed % growth in market value by year =   5%

Part 2 - *Using optimistic but hopefully realistic numbers*

Year 15	Year 20	Year 25	Year 30
425,685	543,294	693,396	884,969
127,086	99,472	62,224	11,982
298,599	**443,823**	**631,173**	**872,987**
16,915	20,954	25,927	32,048
7,492	5,789	3,492	393
6,000	6,000	6,000	-
3,422	**9,165**	**16,436**	**31,655**
1,198	**3,208**	**5,752**	**11,079**
0.35	0.35	0.35	0.35
16,915	20,954	25,927	32,048
(12,375)	(12,375)	(12,375)	(12,375)
4,540	**8,579**	**13,553**	**19,673**
1,198	3,208	5,752	11,079
3,342	**5,371**	**7,800**	**8,594**
0.078	0.125	0.181	0.200
3,342	5,371	7,800	8,594
4,882	6,586	8,883	11,982
20,271	25,871	33,019	42,141
28,495	**37,828**	**49,702**	**62,717**
0.663	0.880	1.156	1.459
210,685	*328,294*	*478,396*	*669,969*
135,825	*168,381*	*190,709*	*199,242*
271,039	*403,076*	*563,719*	*759,166*

NOW LET'S LOOK at a much worse case scenario with almost no growth, same vacancies, more problems, whatever. No growth, by the way, means candy bars and cars would cost almost the same in 30 years as they do today. Good luck with that!

1. Vacancy rate ... **6%**
2. Gross operating income ... **2%**
3. Operating expenses ... **2%**
4. Growth in market value ... **2%**

Remember: If #4 isn't a positive number, don't even think of doing this deal!

Pro Forma Property Analysis - Your First Rental House

Type of Property:	Your First Rental House, with lower expectations	
Location:	Lousy Lane	

	Number of Units	Projected monthly rent / unit
Total Units	1	$1,200
2 Bdrm Units	1	$1,200
1 Bdrm Units	0	$0
Other units	0	$0

Projected annual rental income:	$14,400
Other annual income (Laundry, Fees, etc.):	$0
Scheduled Gross Income	$14,400

Description of Facts

Asking Price:	$215,000	**Land:**	$50,000
Improvements:	$165,000	**Salvage Value:**	0
Asking Price / Unit:	$215,000		

Rentable Sq. Footage:	1500

Depreciation Method:	27.5 years	**Depreciation / year:**	$6,000.00

Proposed Financing

Amount:	$172,000	**N =**	30
Interest Rate:	6.00%	**Annual Payments:**	($12,374.72)
		Monthly Payments:	($1,031)

Part 1 (input) - *Less income, more expenses and lower growth in value over time*

Property Income Statement

Scheduled Gross Income	14,400
(% Vacancy & Credit Losses) 6%	(864)
Gross Operating Income	**13,536**

Less: Operating Expenses

Property Taxes	1,894
Insurance	500
Utilities	-
Licenses / Permits	-
Advertising	-
Management	720
Payroll	-
Supplies	-
Administrative	
Maintenance	1,200
Replacement Reserve	
Total Operating Expenses	**4,314**
Net Operating Income	**9,222**
Capitalization Rate	**0.043**
(Net Operating Income / Market Value)	

Comments:

These examples and calculations are for illustrative purposes only,
and do not reflect actual properties, market values, loans,
operating income or expenses.

Pro Forma Property Analysis - Your First Rental House (results)

	Year 1	Year 5	Year 10
Equity Calculation			
Market Value (Beg)	215,000	232,723	256,945
Less: Total Loans	172,000	162,737	147,559
Owner's Equity	**43,000**	**69,986**	**109,386**
Tax Calculation			
Net Operating Income	9,222	9,982	11,021
Less: Interest	10,263	9,691	8,755
Less: Depreciation	6,000	6,000	6,000
Taxable Income	**(7,041)**	**(5,709)**	**(3,734)**
Income Tax	**(2,464)**	**(1,998)**	**(1,307)**
Income Tax Rate	0.35	0.35	0.35
Cash Flow Calculation			
Net Operating Income	9,222	9,982	11,021
Less: Financing Pmts	(12,375)	(12,375)	(12,375)
Gross Spendable	**(3,153)**	**(2,393)**	**(1,354)**
Less: Income Tax	(2,464)	(1,998)	(1,307)
Net Spendable	**(689)**	**(394)**	**(47)**
Net Spendable Rate	**(0.016)**	**(0.009)**	**(0.001)**
(Net Spendable / Equity)			
Equity Income			
Net Spendable	(689)	(394)	(47)
Plus: Principal Reduction	2,112	2,684	3,620
Plus: Market Value Growth	-	4,563	5,038
Net Equity Income	**1,424**	**6,852**	**8,611**
Net Equity Income Rate	**0.033**	**0.159**	**0.200**
(Net Equity Income / Equity)			
FYI: Accumulative Market Value Growth	-	17,723	41,945
FYI: Total Interest Paid (accumulative)	10,263	49,927	95,687
FYI: Accumulative Gross Operating Income	13,536	70,442	148,215

Notes on Growth Projections:

*Assumed Gross Operating Income % increase by year = 2%

*Assumed Total Operating Expenses % increase by year = 2%

*Assumed % growth in market value by year = 2%

Part 2 - *Less income, more expenses and lower growth in value over time*

Year 15	Year 20	Year 25	Year 30
283,688	313,214	345,814	381,807
127,086	99,472	62,224	11,982
156,602	**213,743**	**283,590**	**369,825**
12,168	13,435	14,833	16,377
7,492	5,789	3,492	393
6,000	6,000	6,000	-
(1,324)	**1,646**	**5,341**	**15,984**
(463)	**576**	**1,869**	**5,594**
0.35	0.35	0.35	0.35
12,168	13,435	14,833	16,377
(12,375)	(12,375)	(12,375)	(12,375)
(206)	**1,060**	**2,458**	**4,002**
(463)	576	1,869	5,594
257	**484**	**589**	**(1,592)**
0.006	0.011	0.014	(0.037)
257	484	589	(1,592)
4,882	6,586	8,883	11,982
5,563	6,141	6,781	7,486
10,702	**13,211**	**16,252**	**17,876**
0.249	0.307	0.378	0.416
68,688	*98,214*	*130,814*	*166,807*
135,825	*168,381*	*190,709*	*199,242*
234,084	*328,889*	*433,562*	*549,130*

NOW COMPARE THE RESULTS of the benefits in 30 years for both examples.

Our most likely example has you with a rental house 30 years from now worth over $800,000 and a positive annual cash flow of over $20,000. By the way, if the renter in this case had stayed in your house for 30 years, they would have paid you over $600,000. We actually have had a tenant stay 26 years in one of our apartments.

Even in the worst case example, in 30 years you have a house worth $300,000+ and a positive annual cash flow of $16,000+. Look at what you put in. The down payment of $43,000 and a negative cash flow that could have lasted between four and almost twenty years. You need to be very aware and very cautious of negative cash flows. Often, they merely present the inconvenience of a forced savings plan with a great payoff; however, if it looks like more than you can handle, don't do the deal. Before you give it up, though, go back to your analysis and look carefully at that negative cash flow. Notice depreciation listed as an expense of $6,000 a year. That's not really an out-of-pocket expense to you, is it? Are you really out $6,000? It could be a real benefit as you make your decision. Look very carefully (Remember: One of the reasons to invest in income property is for "tax savings"). Also look carefully at what the tenants put in over 30 years: everything you didn't. That $500,000+ is called rent, or gross operating income. More importantly, what you have and own is now debt free! The tenant has rent receipts, nothing but rent receipts, period.

Graph 1

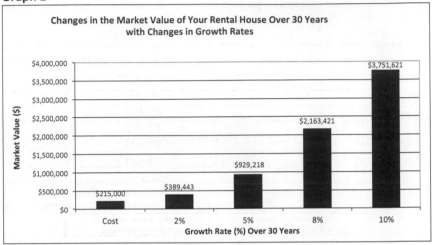

Graph 1 demonstrates the dramatic effect your projected growth rate (appreciation) has on the value of your rental house and thus your net worth. *Don't be overly optimistic when you estimate this rate of growth because it will overshadow the rest of your analysis, even to the point of making a very poor property look good.* It's far better to be overly cautious now and happy with your final results down the road.

Graph 2

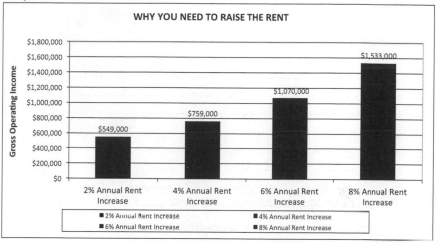

WHY YOU NEED TO RAISE THE RENT

Graph 2 emphasizes the importance of raising rents and staying with the current market rental rates. Notice we didn't say over-raise. To a large extent, the future value of your property and your net worth is determined by the rental income it brings in. Many investors fail here because of their reluctance to raise the rent, falsely thinking they are being nice guys and helping the tenants. If you really want to help the tenants, buy them a copy of this book so they can start saving and invest in their own property.

Graph 3

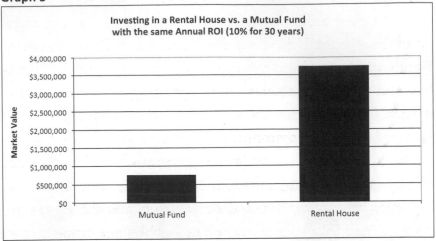

This final graph speaks for itself. Invest your $43,000 in a rental house, take on all the ensuing responsibilities of ownership, and learn how to manage something. OR give your money to a broker, invest in a mutual fund, and hope for the best. We aren't saying don't use mutual funds. What we're saying is that investing in income property is a completely different kind of investment from a mutual fund. So, look carefully at how you plan to achieve your goal of financial independence and what kinds of sustainable, sound investments you need to make to get there.

If 30 years ago you had started spending less than you made and invested in the rental house, you would now own this asset. You would also own the positive income stream from this asset for the rest of your life, or until you sell the property. It doesn't really matter so much *exactly* what happens along the way to that 30-year mark because whatever happens it will be relative to the economic and political environment of the future. Think about that future and the predictions you might have for it. How about population here in the U.S.? Do you think the immigration rate and birth rate will decline? We don't. In fact, we think these are strong underlying trends, and that the population here in the U.S. and the world will only grow, and grow significantly. We think inflation will become a growing problem and that entitlements will be a growing burden. We think natural resources are being depleted at an accelerating rate and that pollution and environmental degradation, especially to the forests and oceans, is already at a dangerous level. These trends of population growth, inflation, entitlements, natural resource depletion and environmental degradation are not short-term cycles. Financial cycles of real estate bubbles and stock market crashes will always impose on these long-term directions. Things in the financial world normally go up and down, and the only way to beat a cycle is to outlast it. Think of business cycles as symptoms of the overall economic and environmental trend of the "new normal," where trust has been damaged and accountability is lacking as you make your personal investment decisions. We will all have to live and invest in the fog of this new normal. You have to make decisions right now under very uncertain circumstances. If you do, you will invest to own something sustainable and have learned how to manage it on the way. If you are paralyzed by the uncertainty, you won't. Just like today, you own something or you don't. You know how to acquire and manage rental property or you don't. If you don't, it doesn't mean you won't. It just means this could be the beginning of your journey toward owning something greater than you do now, and understanding something greater—how to create a sound, sustainable financial future.

Before you start an analysis, make sure you have your facts straight. We are including the following checklist again to emphasize the importance of checking and double-checking your assumptions as you organize information for your investment decision.

Property Analysis Assumptions

The following elements/assumptions need to be addressed in order to complete the income property analysis:

WHAT YOU NEED TO KNOW	WHAT YOU WERE TOLD	WHAT YOU CONFIRMED	DIFFERENCE
BUILDING NAME			
BUILDING ADDRESS			
TOTAL UNITS			
MARKET PRICE			
MARKET PRICE/UNIT			
SQUARE FOOTAGE			
LOAN AMOUNT			
INTEREST RATE			
LOAN PERIOD			
PROJECTED ANNUAL RENT/UNIT			
OTHER ANNUAL INCOME			
SCHEDULED GROSS ANNUAL INCOME			
VACANCY AND CREDIT LOSSES			
GROSS OPERATING INCOME			
(continued next page)			

WHAT YOU NEED TO KNOW	WHAT YOU WERE TOLD	WHAT YOU CONFIRMED	DIFFERENCE
OPERATING EXPENSES:	-	-	
- Property Taxes			
- Insurance			
- Utilities			
- Licenses / Permits			
- Advertising			
- Management			
- Payroll			
- Supplies			
- Services			
- Maintenance			
- Other			
TOTAL OPERATING EXPENSES			
NET OPERATING INCOME			
CAPITALIZATION RATE			
(Net Operating Income / Market Value)			

Analysis Sheet Template and Sample Analyses

After you answer the questions about the property analysis assumptions, and you're confident they are accurate, you are ready to analyze an income property investment of your own. We've included a blank template in the appendix followed by an example analysis of a duplex, four-plex and eight-plex.

What Now? That's Up to You.

You are now armed and dangerous as a real estate investor. Armed with the knowledge of what not to do, and dangerous to both competitors and yourself. You are dangerous to competitors because you will buy good real estate and manage it wisely for long-term gains. You are dangerous to yourself because it is easy to move too quickly and confidently before you let experience teach you how to confront unique situations with wisdom. One of the great characteristics of good leaders, whether they are leading a nation or their own lives, is their understanding of calculated risk. You now need to know your own risk and hassle tolerance in rental real estate terms, and you can only find that out by trying it on an appropriate scale. Sometimes that is a duplex, even one which you inhabit half of. Sometimes it is a multiple-unit rental owned with others. Compatible partners can spread risk and work, and they also spread reward. The point is that you can only find your tolerance level through trial and error, and this makes it imperative to make the errors tolerable. We say start, but start small. We also say start now. The sooner you start, the sooner your "experience capital" will begin to grow.

"In the land of the blind, the one-eyed man is king."

DESIDERIUS ERASMUS

5

Choosing
The Right Partner(s)

What To Do Before You Say "I Do"

WHY HAVE A PARTNER? The short answer is to do something you can't do by yourself. In a partnership you share your strengths in order to reach a common goal. Good partners can make you better. Bad partners will cause problems, so choose wisely. Good or bad, partners always bring something, even if it's only a lesson. Don't look for a partner only because you like them or because you're related to them. Look for partners with qualities that will help you reach your goals. You don't want weak partners that are naive and don't ask questions; you want strong partners with skills that will make you better. The better your partners are, the better you will be. You want partners that expect the same from you. You want clear goals for your partnership and clear expectations that every partner understands and agrees with. Usually when we think of partners, we think of the ones who invest with us, our equity partners.

Having the right partner can be a competitive advantage because it allows you to leverage your skills, time, resources and money. In an ideal partnership, one partner has what the other lacks, which makes the value of the partnership greater than the sum of each individual's contributions. This enhanced value is called synergy. Partners can help you close and manage a deal because they bring what you need to the table. You, in turn, bring what your partner needs.

It is said there is a lot of money out there looking for a home. If your plan is solid, well researched and reasonable, then finding the right partner or the money to do your deal is just another step in your journey. In fact, finding the partner or the money probably isn't nearly as difficult as finding the deal. You see, if the deal is that good, any reasonable person would invest in it and probably be willing to be your equity partner.

When you begin a partnership, you need a shared vision of what you can and will accomplish together. That vision needs synergy. It needs to be the realization of something greater than either of you could or will do on your own. When you're starting to look for income properties, the deals you will be looking at will probably be less than ideal. Experienced investors are looking at the same properties you want and probably before you. Be aware that one of the benefits in your struggle to find better deals may in fact be the synergy of the working partnership itself.

A working partnership means the partners' expectations are met or exceeded. If you can clearly identify your goals, what you bring to the table, and what you expect of your partner, it becomes easier to find deals because you know exactly what you're looking for. You may also find a friend and mentor for life. Like any new experience, however, there will be a learning curve.

The reasons to have a partner are many and vary based on your personal situation and goals. In our lives we use partners constantly to achieve our goals. Successful people are used to working together and partnering on projects. Banks are used to lending and looking to become your financing partner on a good project. So what may seem strange or uncomfortable to you, for them is just the routine leveraging of their time and resources. Usually these partnership efforts are either formal or informal collaborations in a union formed to achieve a specific goal. Even with a binding agreement, the expectations and eventual outcome are largely based on an informal collaboration over time, which in turn determines the success of the partnership.

You may or may not have a contract with the company where you currently work, but the fact that you work there and they pay you means you are (in a sense) a partner. You're the partner the other partner calls an employee. They are the partner you call boss. You may not feel like a partner where you currently work, but we don't care how you feel. What we want to know is what are you going to do about how you feel? If you don't like your work, meaning your current role as an employee, change it. If you can't change it, then supplement it with additional work you do like. Chances are a big part of what you don't like about your job is the fact that you have little to no equity. Meaning you're not an equity partner. Having equity in your work makes bad things tolerable and good things great! If you don't have it where you work, one good way to get equity is owning small residential rental properties. If your long-term goal is to be an owner, to have equity in return for your effort, and you're not getting it where you are now, then you may have to multi-task.

The problem with not being a partner (other than equity issues) usually comes about because of other unmet employment expectations. This often has to do with compensation. When you're working, your compensation package will usually take the form of pay, perhaps with additional perks such as insurance, retirement benefits, security, paid vacations, sick days and maybe even a little personal recognition from time to time. This compensation package is euphemistically called "golden handcuffs." The problem with handcuffs, even golden ones, is they keep you from being free to do the things you want or need to do. Some of the benefits you're getting may in fact not really be that beneficial. First, your total compensation is what you get in return for your work: It's all your money. Your employer is just keeping part of it and calling it a "benefit." By calling compensation a benefit, it makes it sound like a gift. Secondly, those gifts that you're supposed to receive in the future may or may not be there when you need them. Here are a few recent examples of companies that didn't meet their employees' expectations: Lehman Brothers, Enron, Washington Mutual, WorldCom, General Motors, Conseco,

Enronian

Our term for incompetent, corrupt managers like those at Enron, the company that went bankrupt in 2001, losing billions of dollars of shareholders' money. Managers deserving this title and at this level seldom go down without taking many others with them. Imagine your investment of your life savings going from $90 a share to less than $1 in under a year. Then imagine anyone dumb enough not to learn anything from this ... that's Enronian.

Chrysler, Thornburg Mortgage, PG&E and Texaco. You will probably recognize these as the 10 largest bankruptcies in the U.S. The many people who lost their retirement and life savings will certainly recognize them.

When you are working with rental properties, with partners or not, you will usually be compensated from cash flow, which would be considered similar to a salary. You will also be compensated with capital gains when you sell the property because you have equity in it. How much you're compensated is a function of how well your property is performing and the agreement you have with your partner(s). Equity is usually a more critical issue and probably the primary reason you would invest in rental properties. Equity eventually becomes cash flow as rents go up and loans are paid off.

The philosopher Bertrand Russell warned: "Don't mistake wishes for facts." The fact is many of your cash flow needs will be met by the compensation you receive from your employer for your work. Another fact, however, is that equity will not usually come from the same source as your compensation, at least not in an amount sufficient to make you financially independent. So, if you're thinking you'll get along on Social Security and retirement benefits, think again. Fact: Social Security is in trouble right now, over 50% of our workforce doesn't have any private pension coverage, and over 30% doesn't have any savings put away specifically for retirement. This is the good news. There are many people who retired thinking they were financially independent only to find their retirement income gone when the company they worked for went out of business and joined the list of failed companies above. When the old system worked, it worked well. It was "normal" for large organizations to "take care" of their employees when they retired. It's not working so well anymore. Welcome to the *new* normal, where you'd better take care of yourself.

One of my (Glen's) partners was the president of a Fortune 500 company. He retired from a job he was great at and, after growing the company to prosperity, left with good benefits for himself. Within 10 years after he left, the company was bankrupt, and his retirement benefits were gone. Luckily, this story still has a happy ending. As I said, we were partners and the partnership is doing fine. Sure, the bankruptcy hurt him financially, but the benefits he lost were only about half of the capital distribution he gets monthly from our real estate partnership.

Being an employee, even at a good job, but not a real (equity) partner with a meaningful future hit home for me one day in my office at the university. A maintenance man was removing the nameplate from the door next to mine. I had just met the office's new occupant a few days earlier. He was a faculty member who had started that term. Now he was gone and his nameplate was going. He passed away. The number of screws holding your nameplate firmly to your office door, or on the pages of time, should never be the measure of your worth. The way they took his name down didn't seem right. There should have been more. I don't know what more, but more. The fact is that far too often you will have no equity at all in the organization you work for. When the time comes to leave, your name comes off the door and that's it. Maybe the moral of the story is, if you expect equity, don't make the government or an employer your only partners (unless you have a really good partnership agreement).

The Agreement

These days partnership agreements are often replaced by LLCs, but that's a decision for your attorneys to advise you on. For our purposes, we can refer to both as the "partnership agreement." As we have repeatedly pointed out, it can be good to have a partner, but only if you really need one and only if you have a clear agreement. Partnership agreements are legal documents that outline each partner's responsibilities, liabilities, compensation and ownership interests. This is not something you want to do on your own. Always use an attorney and an accountant, and understand everything you are signing. That said, there are two parts to this agreement: the partner's part and the attorney and accountant's part. The partner's part is called the "deal points." These are the critical issues of who does what, gets what and when in the partnership. Your attorney and accountant's part is to make sure your partnership functions for the partners, and functions legally. Your attorney and your accountant can advise you, but they can't know what you want. You and your partner must have your own goals, your own vision of the partnership, your own deal points. This part of the partnership agreement is the arrangement you and your partners have agreed will be not only fair but motivational to all.

Deal points address compensation, if any, who is responsible for what, and who handles the day-to-day activities of the partnership. This could include advertising, showing and renting vacant units, or meeting with property managers (if you have one). Who does the accounting? How is it done? What kind of reports are generated and how often? If additional funds are needed to operate, who supplies them and how much? How is the money you make divided and when? If there is a loss or a gain, how is that divided? Can you sell whenever you want?

Do you have to offer it to your partner first? How long does he have to decide? How is the price determined? What happens if a partner dies or can't do their job? This list goes on and on. It needs to be well thought out and has to blend with the requirements your attorneys and accountants have that will allow your partnership or LLC to function optimally and legally. We won't bore you with all the questions you will need to answer, but we will give you a few tips to help with the process.

Tip #1

Work out the deal points with your partner as much as you can because your attorney and accountant can't and shouldn't decide these things. How would they know who should mow the grass on your rentals? It's also very expensive for you to pay them to sit there and try. If you can't work out the deal points, you don't have a partner. And if you don't have a partner, you don't need a partnership agreement.

Tip #2

Use one attorney and one accountant to make up your partnership agreement or LLC. This will help you avoid a process called "back and forth." In this process, you and your partner-to-be each have your own attorney and your own accountant. You meet with yours and your partner-to-be meets with his, each time sending documents, questions and objections back and forth. This, of course, is done at your expense and can take what seems like forever. Use one attorney and one accountant that both partners feel comfortable with. Let them clarify and refine your vision, sharpen your deal points, ask the questions you both forgot to ask, and get a working agreement. Now you can have everything reviewed by your own attorneys and accountants, but with the caveat that all questions are welcome. Suggestions are also welcome, but only with a written explanation of why they are necessary and essential to the agreement. You're attempting to clarify your deal points by explaining them to someone outside the partnership, someone who is skillful in making these agreements not only legal but work well. If you can compromise and correct the objections of your attorneys and accountants, you will have a solid foundation for your partnership. If you can avoid the back and forth, you will save money. If you don't avoid the back and forth, you will really understand Tip #2.

TIP #3

Not everything in your partnership has to be equal. You may need your partner's money more than he needs your help as the manager, or the other way around. Remember synergy? You want more from doing something together than you could have by each doing the same thing on your own. Perhaps you could individually buy, successfully manage, and profitably sell one rental house, but together as partners you can do the same with six. With synergy, you could both be much better off. However, if your agreement was set up so that your partner received all the profit from five of those houses and you only received profit from one, it wouldn't benefit you because it's probably no better than you could have done on your own.

Having lopsided benefits and risks won't allow your partnership to function well. Ideally, as you negotiate responsibilities and eventual benefits, make your agreement so that each partner benefits most from the success of the other. Too often agreements break down before they begin because of a perceived unfairness. As you negotiate with your partner-to-be, stay flexible and don't let feelings trump facts and goals.

Example: Your partner is willing to do all the work but will put in less money than you. For his work, he thinks capital gains should be divided so you get the gain from two houses and he gets the capital gain from four. There are different ways to think about this offer. It's not 50/50, and you're putting in more money. You could walk away from this. However, you do get the gains from two houses instead of the one you would have gotten on your own, and you don't have to do any of the work for the next 10 or so years until these houses sell. This is a simple way of saying don't be a pig and end up doing nothing. Instead, make a deal that works for everyone.

A friend of ours went into a partnership on a rental house with one of his relatives. His partner/relative put in almost all the money, and our friend agreed to do all the management and repair work, everything from renting vacant units to doing repairs and taxes. The partner/relative did his part, but our friend didn't really keep up his end of the deal. He just wouldn't, couldn't or didn't want to do the work that needed to be done. The partnership failed, a really good opportunity was lost, and a relationship was strained. The point being don't offer to put something into a partnership that you don't have or are unwilling or unable to do. It's critical to the success of your partnership that the partners are capable of their contributions and motivated by the benefits of the partnership, which must be equitable and fair.

TIP #4
Have an exit strategy. You need to plan how the partnership will end: things like you wanting out and how that might happen,

death of a partner and the associated buy/sell options, including first right of refusal and any discount a surviving partner might receive as compared to an outside buyer. These are all things that have to be reviewed in depth by your attorney, accountant and all the partners involved.

TIP #5

One tip we have personally found very useful (and you probably won't be told about) is to include an example calculation of a future sale in the partnership agreement. Basically, this means you should use numbers in addition to words, instead of only words, to explain the key terms and division of profit in your partnership agreement. Ten years from now, it won't be fun when you really have to sell and there is strong disagreement about what certain words in your partnership agreement really mean. Use examples with numbers that all partners agree on, and make it part of your partnership agreement. Use an example of a property you would be interested in being partners on and extrapolate out for, say, 10 or 20 years with the associated increases in value. Then have your accountant divide the proceeds from the hypothetical property sale. This would include a division of cash, operating income and capital gains. When all parties agree on the division of all proceeds, incorporate this example into your partnership agreement as an exhibit. Using examples and having clearly defined terms makes for a much better partnership.

TIP #6

Always do more than expected. Remember the golden rule!

6

Leverage

Using Debt As A Tool

A FUNNY THING ABOUT LEVERAGE is that people often think of it only as analogous to debt, and in turn think of debt as an idea that belongs in a deep hole full of other very bad ideas. The fact is that the word leverage doesn't only mean "financial leverage" and certainly does not just mean debt. Leverage permeates our society and our culture; it can be social, political, religious and professional, as well as financial. Leverage can be the advantage that makes good things better but can also become the problem that makes bad things worse. Any tool used incorrectly won't give the benefits for which it was intended. By accepting the negative connotations that have culturally evolved regarding leverage and debt, we inhibit our ability to use them correctly (as tools) and to our advantage. For example: A normal loan-to-value ratio on a rental property might be 4 to 1, and on the right deal would be a great tool. As the financial crisis unfolded, loan-to-value ratios on mortgage-backed securities were often at 400 to 1 with no hope of generating the cash to cover the debt payments the instant the real estate market stopped going up (as we all know now, it did). In fact, even at the consumer level, banks were more than willing to make highly leveraged home loans with what were referred to as <u>liar's loans</u> (no loan verification, so put anything you want on the application because it won't be checked) or ninja loans (no income, no job and no assets).

It's not unusual to be confused when we think about debt. We may need it but no one wants it. Some of us will try to differentiate between good debt and bad debt. One easy way to make this distinction is to ignore the debt momentarily and think about the spending choices being made. The notion of bad debt usually means debt incurred for the wrong reasons; chief among them is the conspicuous consumption of unnecessary consumer goods. So, sure, if the spending is based on poor choices, then any debt incurred is a poor choice too. But it's obvious that it's really not the debt but rather the spending that's the problem. The negative connotation, however, of all debt being bad debt is widely held and deeply imbedded in the cultural, religious and economic history of our country. Good debt, for those willing to differentiate, is taken on with the rational expectation of improving your situation or because

Liar's Loans

Loans made without any documentation or verification of the information supplied by a buyer. Another common term for this is "ninja loan," meaning the buyer had "No income, No job, No assets" but they still got the loan! Then came the mortgage crisis, income documentation, no more flipping, and they lost their houses.

it is simply necessary. Examples of good debt include things like home loans or school loans and usually have one clear distinction—a specific and measurable repayment plan for a reasonable spending choice. Important distinction though it is, our personal opinions and fears about debt need to be separated from and carefully compared to our understanding and use of leverage as a management and investment tool.

Good debt, as contrasted to bad debt, is a consumer concept and somewhat subject to the rationalization of the consumer. Instead of being a tool, it becomes an opinion or construct. Comparing bad debt with a bad investment may help. Often thought of as analogous, they are actually quite different. For the most part, bad debt is a function of its use and not its amount; therefore, by definition it becomes a construct.

EXAMPLE: You already have $20,000+ in credit card debt you're having trouble paying off. You see a really cute purse that you definitely need. You buy that purse before you pay off those credit cards and that's bad *debt*.

A bad *investment* only becomes bad when bad isn't priced into the cost of the investment; therefore, by definition it becomes a mistake.

EXAMPLE: You find a house for sale for $200,000 and buy it, only to find out later there was $75,000 of damage to the foundation. You missed the damage in your inspection and it has to be repaired immediately. The investment is bad because the $75,000 wasn't priced in. You should theoretically have gotten the house for $125,000. Paying $200,000 was a mistake. The problem, of course, is knowing what *bad* is and how to know when it's priced in.

How can debt-dependent questions like what home or what school or what consumer goods (for that matter) be analyzed from a management point of view when they are personal decisions based on personal opinions and personal choices? There are plenty of rules of thumb and common sense ideas that help consumers make wiser choices about using debt for consumer purchases. You may have a fuzzy line of thinking between different types of consumer debt, like student loans that were necessary and credit card debt that allowed you to spend more than you made, but you know if you're in the group of over-spending train wrecks addicted to consumer spending. If you don't care to be in this group, then don't. You'll need to get your personal finances in order, have a financial plan, stop using debt for consumer purchases you really can't afford, and understand exactly how leverage (as a tool) can help you with this plan.

Leverage is defined as the advantage or power gained by using a lever. It can also be explained as the ability to use influence to affect people, events, outcomes and decisions. The historical development, or etymology, of the word comes from the Latin verb *levare*, meaning "to lighten." When we invest and use debt to increase the return on an investment, it's called financial leverage. This is probably the reason leverage is commonly equated with debt. If we were to adjust the definition slightly and say that "leverage is the power gained by using an advantage," we would have a more modern, useful and functional definition for our real estate investments. This definition would also emphasize the use of all kinds of leverage, including financial leverage, as contrasted with the negative associations of being in debt.

For example: Our country is in debt right now, as are many people in this country. That's not leverage, it's just debt. The word *debt* developed from the vulgar Latin word *debita*, "that which is owed." As you can see, <u>leverage is a tool; debt is a condition</u>. And as the song says, we need to be careful about what condition our condition is in.

Every deal has two parts—price and terms—and leverage is important to both. A buyer with more cash might have an advantage on price over a buyer that has to sell another property first or line up financing. A long-term banking customer might have an advantage with terms over a buyer with no history at the bank where they seek financing. These advantages can be considered a type of leverage.

Leverage exists everywhere in business. When a company installs self-checkout machines, it creates operating leverage. Operating leverage, then, is when a company purchases equipment that initially raises its fixed costs and breakeven point in order to lower its variable costs. It does this knowingly because once it reaches the new breakeven point, more of every sales dollar will go to profit. It goes to profit because there is no more checkout person and thus no more medical insurance, no more sick days and no more vacations for that employee. All these employee-associated expenses are known as variable costs: the checkout people (variable cost) have been replaced by a machine (fixed cost) that works 24/7. Fewer checkout people equal more profit.

In real estate investment, financial leverage is not only common but usually necessary, especially when you're new to investing in income property. Financial leverage is necessary first because of large capital costs, but equally and more importantly because of the need to increase the return on the investment. Let us explain.

Let's look at an example of a duplex you're interested in. Assuming you have carefully and accurately figured out your income, expenses, appreciation, how you're going to manage it, and have negotiated the best possible price, now you have to do something: You have to buy it!

Is it wise to pay cash even if you have it and get X return that includes after-tax cash flow and appreciation? Or should you finance the property, given that it still has a very positive <u>debt service ratio</u> and cash flow (which means your net operating income more than covers your debt service)? The answer is usually easy. Assuming you have a normal loan-to-value ratio for the property, say 80% loan and 20% equity, you could buy four more properties with the cash you have, making your return five times what it is on the single property. This is a hard tool not to use. Done right you've increased your return by five times,

Debt Service Ratio

The debt service, or coverage, ratio is the ratio between the annual NOI and the annual debt service (NOI / Debt Service). This is a widely used measure to determine that the income from your property is sufficient to pay the mortgage payments, so leave yourself some room and cash flow. If this ratio is less than 1, then you have a negative cash flow and most responsible lenders won't/shouldn't make this loan. What's the solution? Put more cash down to lower the mortgage payments or get the seller to lower the price. Once you get the income up, you can refinance and get some or all of your cash out.

and it could also mean you can buy the property with much less cash and get into it much sooner, perhaps one-fifth of the time a cash purchase would take. You're using financial leverage and you may have increased the return on your investment. It makes the decision easy, but be cautious when it makes it too easy. You have to remember to be careful because leverage is a sword that cuts both ways. While it can magnify your return, it can also magnify your losses. Every mistake you make is magnified by leverage if you're wrong about any of the projections you made regarding income, expenses and appreciation. Leverage also has a time component. Long-term assets need to be financed with long-term debt. There are countless examples of "good" real estate deals with incorrect financing, where the property was lost because balloon payments couldn't be met. The problems with bad timing are just as bad as the problems of too much leverage. Once you buy the property, those projections are yours to live with. Those aren't just numbers on paper anymore. They are expectations, and promises you made. You're the manager now, and making those numbers happen is your responsibility.

In the business of real estate investment, decisions must be based on evidence. This means evidence needs to be collected and analyzed in order to make a responsible decision, a process called <u>due diligence</u>. The more accurate and complete the evidence, the better the analysis. The better the analysis, the better the outcome of the investment can be.

Consumer decisions and purchases tend to be less analytical. They present more risk and immeasurable (less quantifiable) returns. This doesn't mean consumer purchases are bad. It means there is usually little or at best unreliable return as an investment. Because of this unreliability, debt used in a consumer purchase or with a consumer mindset becomes a much greater

Due Diligence

The process of evaluating everything possible about your potential income property investment: not just the price, income and expenses, but answering questions about everything from zoning to title insurance, deferred maintenance, structural defects, building code violations, future repair costs and environmental concerns, just to name some of what due diligence means for you. We almost bought an apartment building that was on the site of an old gas station with buried gas tanks ... big problem and definitely a "deal killer" unless that cleanup is priced in. Investors commonly buy rental houses only to find old, buried oil tanks that they become responsible for. Due diligence means measure twice, cut once.

risk with a number of negative consequences. We have all seen the terrible consequence to our economy and the world's economy of too much debt. We've also seen the problems caused by the consumer mindset that falsely predicted home prices only go up and things only improve for investors and homeowners.

As witnessed in the disastrous economic results of 2007, there is a difference between evidence and deception, analysis and fabrication, due diligence and deliberate fraud. Even for business, debt used inappropriately isn't leverage. At best it's still just bad debt, too much fuzzy thinking. Remember: Leverage is a tool; debt is a condition. The reversal of Glass-Steagall in 1999 set off a tiering of many layers of debt in the banking industry with little to no regulation or transparency. What was euphemistically passing as "business decisions" from 1999 to 2007 (when our financial meltdown was finally exposed), in reality didn't ever meet the standards of being evidence-based or reasonable. What passed for blame was the notion that investors and home buyers had become complacent and that regulators became overwhelmed. It's fairly apparent now that there was no accountability and it was the regulators who were complacent. The investors and homeowners were misled by abusive and deceptive lending practices, such as the "no documentation" loans. For those involved in this deception, to blame this entire problem on overleveraged investments in toxic assets is an insult to bad investments everywhere. The fact is it wasn't the assets that were toxic. The management and oversight of the leverage were toxic.

Leverage, again, is a tool just like a hammer is a tool. You can't reasonably hit someone in the head with a hammer and blame the hammer. You also can't purposefully ignore due diligence, hide facts (called limited transparency by those who benefited from it), and leverage your "structured products" (CDOs and CMOs) at 400 to 1 and blame leverage. It will be an interesting process as time uncovers the fingerprints on this hammer. The fingerprints may become more visible as we find out who got paid based on loan volume, and how much of this "pay" was put into identifiable political contributions to keep the deception going. It seems the ones who benefited the most would like everyone to believe that this financial disaster was no one's fault, that there is equal blame for all—the government for allowing it to happen, the predatory mortgage banking industry for exploiting it, and finally the "greedy" homeowners for not being more careful. That being the case, why not have the government pick up their third of every bad loan for their self-admitted responsibility and the banks do the same. That leaves our troubled or toxic loans at one-third of their original balance. Probably some of the so-called "greedy" homeowners can then be responsible for their fair share of the mess but keep their homes and their dreams. But that is for a different book. Our purpose here isn't to assign blame for what happened between 1999 and 2007, but rather to put it in perspective and explain the reasonable use of debt to make management decisions for the Next Generation. In order to put our finances in order and take advantage of investment opportunities that come along in real estate or anything else, it will be important that financial leverage is used with respect and not avoided because of fear. Using leverage with respect and due diligence will allow you to become a hands-on manager making deliberate investment decisions as opposed to the resigned acceptance of loss experienced by the passive and misled investor of 2007.

But we are not finished with leverage yet.

Think of leverage as a stick. You use the long end of it to lift or pry something you otherwise couldn't. Now think of that stick as time—the longer you wait to use it, the shorter your stick will be. By starting to invest early in life, you have time on your side. The benefits of compound interest are amazing, but they require time. Invest $1,000 at 10% for 10 years and it grows to almost $3,000. But let it grow for 50 years, and it grows to almost $120,000. In order for your money to work for you (instead of only the other way around), you need a plan and you need time. If you need, say, $50,000 a year to live comfortably and you can still earn, say, 10% on your investments, then of course you need $500,000. That means your nest egg of $500,000 is earning the $50,000 a year you need to live comfortably. Well, if you're 65 now, all you had to do was put away about $4,000 when you were 15, never touch it, and you would almost be all set. But most of us either wouldn't or couldn't do this for whatever reason. If we ever do put something away, we touch it (i.e., spend it). So we end up short on time and money, a situation commonly known as "a day late and a dollar short."

The Three-Legged Stool

A remedy to this problem could be to think of our solution as a three-legged stool. Each leg on our stool is a different type of leverage. The first leg is financial leverage, which can magnify your return on investment. You'll need this when you become short on time. The second leg of the stool is to leverage our time with our saving and investment discipline, which involves choosing an investment we cannot easily touch when we only think we may need it or (even worse) think we want something else more. The key word here is *easily*. That really makes this second leg sound awful; however, if we carefully examine the reasons most people never reach their financial goal or financial independence, we see it's often because they don't have the discipline to save and/or invest over a long period of time. So here we are leveraging our time by changing our discipline. We change our discipline by converting some of our assets from liquid to illiquid. Assets will now be at the bottom of our balance sheet instead of only at the top. So whether it's a business you own or a small income-producing property as we suggest, you'll now have assets (equity) at the bottom of your balance sheet that require discipline and management skills. Imagine you're sitting around a campfire and your liquid assets are your kindling and your fixed assets are your logs. It's hard to start a fire with logs and you can't keep a good fire going with just kindling.

Finally, for the third leg, we leverage our work and skills against our problems. Of course, this requires recognizing the skills we may or may not have and correctly identifying our problems and weaknesses. In short, we need to become managers of our investments and leverage our management skills.

Let's return to the earlier duplex example and list how this kind of three-legged leverage might work to your advantage, even with obstacles.

EXAMPLE: You have found a property that is a really good deal and you have the time, skills and energy to make this property a successful investment. However, you don't even have enough money for the down payment (a very common problem). Don't worry. You don't need all the money. You only need enough for the down payment and enough equity to ensure you have an ongoing positive cash flow. One possible solution: Find a partner! Find one that can strengthen your weaknesses. You know what you need from the partner: money and the skills in finance, accounting and management that probably go with it. The question is what does the partner need from you? Chances are they need you to be the "subject matter" partner, which means you have a keen understanding of this property, will manage the investment, and do all the day-to-day work to maximize its value (another very common problem). Your future partner usually solves this problem by hiring an employee. Just as you will need (and get) more than just money from your partner, they must need you to do more than the day-to-day work of an employee. They need you to find, negotiate, acquire, manage, monitor and dispose of the investment. This job is different. This time you want more than income; you want ownership. Your position is different too because you're responsible for the outcome. You don't want to be just an employee. You want to be a partner. For you this may be the first time in your life when someone wanted what you have to offer and was willing to offer you something more than just a paycheck. This time, the offer is for income and equity. You need your partner for the same reasons they need you: to do what the other can't or won't and to increase their return on investment and net worth (equity).

"It's not what you make, it's what you keep."

What you keep is your equity, and equity is critical to your future success.

Objection: But you said find a partner that has what you need and needs what you have, and then you say that you and your partner both need the same thing. This doesn't make sense.

Answer: Actually, it makes perfect sense. Recall Chapter 5. You and your partner had different needs going into the investment, but you had the same long-term goals for its success. Think about it. In the long term you both wanted to increase your net worth (equity) and to increase the return on your investment. You increased the return on your investment of *work*, with maybe some small amount of the required money and most of the management. Your partner put in most of the money but didn't have to do much of the work. He increased the return on his investment of *money*. You both increased your equity leverage by having the tenants pay down your mortgage and having the property appreciate over time. You may have even traded up (1031 exchange) to larger and more successful properties over time or borrowed against the equity in your investment to buy additional properties. You formed a partnership that spelled out what you expected of each other, how you were each being compensated, and how profits and capital gains from your joint venture would be divided. You both did something that helped you in the way you each needed help. You both leveraged your time. You both successfully leveraged your skills. You both successfully increased your financial leverage.

You needed to remedy a problem. The problem was achieving financial independence and not having enough time, money, or both to do it. This example would be but one of many remedies for that problem. First, you increased your use of financial leverage by trading management responsibilities for the cash you didn't have. Second, you leveraged your time and investment discipline by investing in income property, which is very illiquid, and also by doing it with a partner, which makes it even more illiquid. Third, you leveraged your skills against your problems. You didn't have the money, but you were willing and able to do the work and you also found a partner who needed what you had—a willingness to make it happen.

Can it go wrong? Unfortunately, yes. Remember the story we recounted earlier of the acquaintance of ours who had asked for advice regarding a real estate deal? If you recall, he explained that he didn't have much money, but he had a friend willing to put almost all the money in to get a rental property they found. We gave him our advice, similar to the advice we're giving you, and they formed a partnership and bought the property. Sadly, it didn't work out. Within a year, they had to sell at a loss. It wasn't because the guy with the money didn't hold up his end of the bargain. Once they bought the property, it was our acquaintance (the one with no money) who decided he was just too busy and couldn't be bothered with all the work involved in managing the property. Why repeat this story? Because leverage, as we have said over and over, is just a tool. It won't help you if you don't do your part. Here was a person who had the chance of a lifetime—to really build equity and work with a friend—and he threw it away. Remember an important fact about leverage: If you're too lazy to push on your end of the lever, it probably won't work.

Leveraging your skills and resources may seem daunting, like searching for a needle in a haystack. The question is how? First, it sounds like you may need a partner who you trust at a very high level. Second, the partner must have needs that are compatible with and complimentary to your problems and needs. How do you find a partner like this? Well, maybe you don't need to. Fact is maybe your first investment should be on your own because then you would have something tangible—a track record—to offer a future partner. You can work and save the money for your down payment. You've probably had to save for other things you've wanted, right? But, back to the question. How do you find a partner? If you have a *good* track record and you find a *good* deal, and the only thing you need to make it work is money, then finding a partner won't be a problem.

Never have a partner if you can do it yourself. Make sure you need an equity partner. It's possible you don't. Instead of a partner, you may wish to first find a mentor, someone to help leverage your skills, and then a deal you do on your own to gain experience. For a mentor, find someone that is successful at what you would like to be successful at too. In this case it's investing in income property. While it may be difficult to find a partner, you may be surprised at how easy it is to find a mentor.

As a business student in graduate school, I (Glen) was often told to find a mentor. It wasn't until later—while teaching finance at the university, when I'd decided to start my own investment advising business—that I understood the wisdom of this advice. There was a marketing professor in our department who had started his own company, ran it successfully, took it public and retired at just the perfect time. He was financially well-off and was only teaching while he looked for another company to start. He was a great teacher, businessman and speaker. After many requests, he agreed to meet with me for lunch once a month so I could pick his brain and get his input on the unbelievable number of problems I was having starting my business. At first he was reluctant, but after a while we became friends and I think he really liked being able to help me. I believe that most people are willing to help someone who really wants to help themselves.

Remember the three-legged stool:

    1. **Learn**: Leverage your skills.

    2. **Start early**: Leverage your time.

    3. **Be careful**: Use financial leverage wisely and leverage your financial resources.

"Price is what you pay. Value is what you get."

Warren Buffett

7

Management Q & A

Lessons from
the Real (Estate) World

MANAGING YOUR INVESTMENT PROPERTY is, as they say, "where the rubber meets the road." Once you make an investment, supervision and management of the property is your responsibility. You have the power to make decisions, and for the most part your objectives are clear. There are laws, regulations and competition that will guide your decisions, but there will be questions. Here we address some of those questions to help you avoid common problems and mistakes in the dynamic, competitive and constantly changing environment of property rental. The counsel we give you is to use common sense and uncommon care. Have the best legal, accounting, management and insurance backup you can, and choose carefully. After all, stuff happens …

WHEN I BUY A RENTAL PROPERTY, SHOULD I HIRE
A MANAGEMENT COMPANY OR DO IT MYSELF?

Good question. The answer is maybe. You will often have to use a property management company simply because your property is just too far away. For now, though, let's assume you're close to your property and have the time (and desire) to manage it yourself, and examine some of the things that will need to be done now that you're an owner. Think about all the things a good property manager can do for you and then ask yourself: "Who can do it better—you or a professional property manager?" Let's define "better" in terms of the value of your time compared to the cost of hiring a management company to get you a comparable return on your investment.

Renting your property means advertising the vacancy, taking the calls, showing the property, screening applicants (avoiding the bad ones), filling out all the paperwork correctly (the lease being just one of those), and collecting your money, all of which has to be done in compliance with state and federal law, as well as local regulations. It seems there are strong arguments for hiring a property manager, but there are also reasons to be very cautious, such as conflicts of interest and excessive costs. Any good property manager could write a book just on this paragraph, explaining the problems they've had and those you're going to have. If you decide to use a property manager, you need a good one because it's far better to do without than have a bad one.

When you're starting out, we believe you need to be involved at the tenant level and need to manage your own property as much as is practical. The reason for this is so you will have experience from the ground level up and make yourself a better owner, investor and eventually client to a good property manager. Your relationship with your property managers will only improve when your expectations are clear, reasonable and based on experience. As your time becomes more valuable, perhaps being used in the acquisition of more property, it *may* become reasonable to gradually turn the day-to-day responsibilities over to professional managers.

We have used good and bad property managers. When you select one, use the same common sense, but even more due diligence, than you would use to select any contractor that is working with your property. Look at their licensing, experience, references, recommendations and how they respond to you. Carefully examine any contract you're asked to sign, and make sure your attorney reviews it as well. Have a way out if things aren't working out to your satisfaction. Carefully review all charges or mark-ups on services you may incur and ask questions about any concerns you may have regarding conflict of interest. Ask for a sample of the type of accounting statement you will be receiving and how any and all of their charges will be listed. Have that reviewed by your accountant. In addition, find out who will be working on, with or in your property, and how they have been screened, as well as how future employees will be screened.

WHAT SHOULD I DO WHEN A TENANT CAN'T PAY THEIR RENT AND ASKS TO LET THEM PAY LATER?

This is almost always a *bad* idea. The nature of a business transaction is quid pro quo—I'm giving you something and you're giving me something back that we both agree is of equal value. In our business, we give you a place to live and you give us money. When you manage your own properties, you will often be asked to change something about the way you run your business. Usually it will be about the rent, but not always. Our opinion, having done this for 35 years, is that it is a mistake to do financial favors (e.g., letting people not pay rent or pay it much later).

First, you don't really know the person. It should strike you as odd that they're an adult and you are the only person in the whole world they know to ask for this assistance. They've probably already alienated every other person in the world they knew!

The most common occurrence is that they can't pay their rent "right now." Well, you have a choice, and it's a hard choice: trust them or evict them. We can tell you with some considerable experience that 100% of the times we trusted them, it worked out badly. It's not uncommon for our new on-site managers to have considerable empathy for the plight of the tenant who can't pay their rent. It's usually because there's a "really good story." We always invite our managers to use their own money if they want, but ours is not available. It's amazing how quickly their empathy evaporates.

We always explain the following to our new resident managers: By allowing tenants to live in our property without paying rent, they enable the person's bad behavior by rewarding it. Most likely, they can count on seeing it again. On the other hand, if they refuse to listen to the excuse and instead start whatever their reasonable legal options are—usually a 72-hour notice and filing for eviction—they will have a much better result: the tenant pays their rent and late fees, doesn't do it again, and there is much less work for us and the manager. A much better result, right? If they really care about this tenant, then this is the kind of behavior they should reward—responsible behavior.

However, if you're like most managers (human), you're likely to get soft at some point and give in. Here's a story (one of many) of when we got soft and didn't follow our own advice.

We had a foreign student that not only couldn't pay his rent, but became upset and downright ugly when asked. Because he was from another country, we tried every possible way to help him, including moving him to a less expensive apartment. Numerous times he didn't show up to agreed upon meetings to pay his rent, so finally we filed in court to have him evicted. This, of course, made him not only angry but verbally abusive to our resident manager. How did it go in court, you ask? Well, he showed up (they often don't). He explained to the judge all the troubles going on in his home country and apologized over and over to us. He also explained that everything could be worked out if he just had two more weeks. The judge explained that he couldn't allow it, so it was up to me. One problem was that if I agreed, I would have to go back to court if he didn't pay. Well, I agreed. He seemed so sincere. No, he never paid. Yes, I had to go back to court. He finally left the apartment an hour before the police were to show up and carry him out. He owed months of rent that we would never see.

IF I GET A BAD CHECK, WHAT SHOULD I DO?

You mean *when* you get a bad check? It's very common that a tenant will bounce their check and then try to give you another check … which of course will also bounce! Just because you got a check doesn't mean you got paid! Each time you take a check, it takes about two weeks to process before you get it back and can react. This becomes a very effective way for a tenant (who either can't or won't pay their rent) to manage their cash flow problems at your expense. Always get cash, a cashier's check, or a money order once you are in a bad check situation.

On each side of my desk, I (Glen) have a frame containing $25,000 in bounced checks. Yep, $50,000 total. Seems like a lot, right? Actually that's a small fraction of the bounced checks we have received; I could easily wallpaper most of my office. Don't ever take a check in payment for a bounced check!

Also, don't take less than you're owed (unless the tenant is on their way out the door and you're positive it's all you will ever get). We lost a very large amount of unpaid rent from a commercial tenant who was a master of avoiding payment and going to court. One of his main strategies was paying partial rent. When the tenant is successful at getting you to accept partial rent, he usually invalidates your lease for that rental period. Here's how it works: He comes in and gives you part of the rent. You take it on the promise that he will bring the rest "soon" or "at the end of the week." Of course, he never does. You go to court and the judge explains there is nothing he can do this month because you invalidated the lease by accepting partial payment. You will have to re-file again next month if he doesn't pay then (at your expense, of course). This guy finds your wife the next month and gives her part of the rent, which she unknowingly accepts and cashes, pushing you back another month. The rent on this space was $3,500 a month. It took eight months to get him out. The lost rent and legal cost came to almost $50,000. Be careful, very careful. One more time … Don't take less than you're owed (unless the tenant is on their way out the door and you're positive it's all you will ever get).

Do you sometimes get frustrated working with tenants and feel there's just nothing you can do?

Yes. Not often, but yes. Most folks you rent to are good people. When I first started investing in rental property, I thought our problems would be with about 5% of the people we rented to. After 30 years, I've adjusted that number up slightly but not much. Most folks are honest, easy to work with, take care of your property, respect you, and pay their rent on time. Having said that, there are problems with the other 5% or so, some of which defy understanding.

We had a tenant that always paid late and I mean *always*! We tried to explain the additional cost to him and the inconvenience to us of having to do this month in and month out. He was very hard to work with, but he lived in an apartment that was generally difficult to rent, so we weren't anxious to have a vacancy. At one point we actually offered him a free month's rent at the end of his contract if he would pay on time each month. He said he was excited to try. Of course he didn't make it a month. When he finally moved, it was because he had stolen the rent money from his wife and she finally left him. She had driven him to the resident manager's apartment to drop off the rent and watched him walk up to the rent box to drop it in. When we called about the late rent, she was adamant that it had been dropped off. When she checked with the bank, she found out what happened to the rent money. He made her believe he put it in the rent box but actually put it in his pocket, cashed it, and gambled it away. That was enough for her *and* us—too many times in court and too many excuses. As they say, it takes all kinds.

What should be done regarding personal items left in an apartment after a tenant has vacated?

They all leave something behind and it's not often a Thank You note. They leave money (sometimes bags of it ... which is great), clothes, jewelry, personal papers and pictures, cars, guns, friends, pets, and often just dirt. When a tenant leaves something behind, remember it's not yours. You are required by law and moral decency to get it back to them if it has any financial or personal value. If you can't get it to them, it still doesn't belong to you. You'll need to check local laws and housing regulations for the legal options available to you for disposing of this property. Chances are they have also left behind damage. You can often sell their property if it has any value to reimburse yourself for any losses, but you have to do so correctly.

Remember, too, that whatever you do, there are some people that will always disagree. One of our properties is a rooming house close to a university and is rented only to students. Often these will be foreign students. One graduate student from Kenya lived there less than a year before he had to leave school and return home. He left no forwarding address. His room was clean but there were a few old textbooks on the floor of his closet. We threw them out. Remember, we're writing these stories so you won't be too surprised when you start dealing with tenants. Two years after he moved out, he came back. And he wanted to know ... that's right ... Where are my books? He was very angry when he found out they were gone and couldn't understand why we would do something like that. What should you do?

Sometimes they leave everything. A woman at one of our apartments in Oregon was late on her rent shortly after the tragedy of 9/11. Her story was that she had lost two family members in the towers. She lived in a one bedroom with a young daughter and a cat. Everyone in the country was still in shock, as were we, and this seemed a reasonable reason to mess up and miss your rent payments. So we let it slide and asked her to contact us as she worked things out and of course sent our condolences. The weeks passed with no word. When we were finally able to reach her, we were informed that she had just been diagnosed with cancer. What do you say? We tried to ask what she would like us to do ... and got no answer. But as is usually the case, the answer came. A few nights later she fought with a neighbor and emptied her cat's litter box from the third floor onto the neighbor's car. This got the police involved. Over the next few weeks, the cat was removed by the Humane Society and the child, soon after, by children's services ... thankfully! We started eviction immediately. There were, of course, no relatives in the towers and no cancer. True her problems may have been almost as bad, but they were well beyond the scope of anything not paying rent could fix. She didn't leave voluntarily. It took lots of time, money and energy in court. The police finally had to physically remove her from the apartment. She left all her belongings, papers and pictures—everything, everything she had in the world.

We are responsible for going through a tenant's belongings in this case, boxing and storing what we think is of value. We tried every way possible to get her to go through the apartment and take whatever she wanted. She wanted nothing. After we worked for days cleaning the apartment and going through her things, she called. She wanted to know if we had found $20 under her mattress. We told her no. She never returned to claim her belongings, and we never heard from her again.

Sometimes, fortunately not often, you have to deal with fairly severe mental health issues. We had another tenant at a different complex live with us for a number of years. Clean cut, single guy, mid to late 30s, good job, nice car, he was always pleasant to everyone. Unknown to us for quite some time, he had real mental problems. The problems became apparent because of smells coming from the apartment and complaints by neighbors. By the time we got him out, it was awful.

Our onsite manager wouldn't even go into the apartment, but I (Glen) wanted to see it. I guess I *needed* to see it but still couldn't believe it. It was the worst case of hoarding and filth I have ever seen. As I entered the apartment, the garbage sloped up to head high. Furniture and garbage bordered a narrow pathway through the living room. In one bedroom, probably where he slept, there was a bare mattress on the floor surrounded by garbage. The other bedroom was even worse. The garbage was waist deep.

The bathroom was filthy beyond imagination. We had to walk on garbage and filth to get into it. To help you visualize, imagine sitting on the toilet and having your feet and butt almost level with the filth and debris on the floor. There were smells that made your skin crawl and a lingering wetness on everything. The tub slim had to be cleaned with a shovel before it could be washed. He left his contact lens cases and cleaners. I remember wondering how he avoided eye infections in that pigsty (believe me, this was an insult to pigs everywhere). The kitchen had debris packed tightly on the floor to the same level as the counter and table top. Again, *so* not good.

Then I made a big mistake. Without thinking, I opened the refrigerator. I guess he was a hunter because the fridge was full of rotten meat. The electricity had been off and the smells that came out were truly so bad I can't even begin to describe them. They seriously could only be measured by the speed that I got out of there.

It took two 30-yard dumpsters to haul away his garbage. Everything in the apartment had to be disinfected, painted, repaired or replaced. I hope he got help, and I truly hope you never have to deal with a problem like this. If you do, be kind but don't avoid it. That would only make it worse for everyone. Remember: Your job is to handle problems.

WHAT ABOUT PETS?

Pets aren't usually the problem. The problem is their owner. One big problem is that tenants will often bring a pet into the unit without telling you. Catch this one right away and save yourself a lot of grief. Our problem with pets is that any damage they do is not usually covered by our insurance. Because this damage can be considerable, we will have to look to the pet's owner for reimbursement, so we want to be sure to screen them prior to accepting them as tenants. Damages can range from the obvious physical damage caused by chewing, scratching, urination and defecation to insect infestation, noise, smells and physical attacks. If they have fish, what happens if the aquarium breaks and floods their apartment? Who is responsible? Who is responsible if it floods the unit below them? Pet problems can be considerable, time consuming, and difficult to prove. They can also cause serious problems for other tenants, which can lead to vacancies for you.

So the question becomes: Why rent to people with pets at all? Well, it makes it easier to rent the property, and usually at a higher rent with increased deposits. In general, if you have a rental that's easy to rent, don't take pets. New carpets? Don't take pets. However, the harder it becomes to rent a unit, the more flexible you must become. When you increase the rent on an apartment and charge a pet deposit, you may recover enough to replace the carpet when your tenant and their pet leave. Just make sure your pencil is sharp and you have figured out what that damage will usually be. I have also found it's much easier to get money from pet owners before they move in than after they leave. People who don't take care of their pets certainly won't take care of their responsibilities to you. Remember: It's always better to have a vacancy than a bad tenant. A vacancy just means no income, whereas a bad tenant means no income, lots of problems, usually damage to the unit, and probably court. The pet is just one more reason you shouldn't have rented to this person in the first place.

IS THAT ALL?

No, not even close. Think about it: Destructive tenants, tenants that become ill, injured, disabled, go missing, or die, flooding and fires, time in court, threats and anger (God only knows from whom or why), abandoned cars, bikes and everything else, including pets, irresponsible tenants and co-signers who are worse, good tenants with bad friends, bugs, bats, mice, lockouts, lockouts in the middle of the night, lockouts where you let the wrong person in, fighting roommates, insect infestations, furniture in the swimming pool, all your flower pots in the swimming pool, naked people in the swimming pool, fussy tenants, theft of your property, theft of your tenant's property, regulations and laws that make no sense, tenants with drug problems (Did you know bedrooms and closets can be converted into marijuana farms or dog kennels?), leaking roofs, broken everything, more bounced checks, and we still aren't even close to listing all the problems you could potentially have.

So why invest in rentals? Because even after all of the problems and horror stories, there is a tremendous investment upside. Because most people you rent to are honest and nice. Because whatever you do in life, you will have problems and horror stories; you just may not be getting compensated for taking care of them. Because most of the management problems you may have can be avoided by being careful and reasonable. Learn about the resources available to you, like professional real estate investment associations that promote professional management practices and offer classes and advice. Have the professional support you need. Again, that means good legal, accounting, insurance, management, and repair backup.

The single most important responsibility you will have is to take care of your property and tenants. Treat your tenants like you would want to be treated. This brings up our "Kids Rule." Take pride in your investment. Don't rent anything out you wouldn't want your own kid to rent, and don't treat a tenant differently than you would want your own child treated.

We hope you see something in our experiences and stories that will help you as you ride the learning curve of investing in small residential income properties. Remember: Common sense and uncommon care. Choose carefully. You may lose on an investment, but you will never lose what you learn.

Concluding Thoughts & Beginning Plans

IN THIS CHAPTER WE TRY TO DISTILL a few key lessons from the preceding seven for building an investment philosophy and skill set, and to make clear (in a small space) the opportunity that diversification provides—moving away from only liquid assets and into fixed assets, such as the right real estate investment. Especially because of the recent recession, we think now is a good time to stop treating ongoing investment cycles as emergencies where you are constantly digging out of another hole trying to regain lost ground. The alternative is to see your financial future for what it is: potential opportunities and potential problems. Often the problems are chronic and might be best resolved, at least in part, with some investment in long-term, income-producing fixed assets like small rental properties. Over and over we have emphasized that your best investment is always to invest in yourself and cultivate the points of perspective that have outcomes with reasonable and proven results. It's not a lofty goal to start applying life leadership to an investment philosophy, particularly for young people. Think of it this way: the problems of owning income property will constantly force you to work on being a better manager, and who are you working for? Yourself! You're an entrepreneur! In addition, because nothing in real estate happens overnight, you have an investment that's harder to sell when it's doing poorly or when you need to. When you don't need to sell and/or it's doing well, you don't want to sell. Real property is so illiquid that you usually either can't or don't want to sell it, so the very nature of the investment gradually forces you to give the time-value of money a chance and to give yourself the opportunity to evolve into a better manager of your own investments over the long run.

As we have seen, our relationship with uncertainty can and will work against us when we make emotional investment decisions. It is normal to feel uncertain and fearful. The financial future *is* uncertain, and the current financial system is sick. But in life, we make mistakes and learn from them. You'll have your share of mistakes and hidden obstacles as well if you're successful with income property investing. When you make a mistake, and you will, just try not to repeat it.

As individuals responsible for our own investment success, we need to make changes and we need to start making them *now*. The old path to financial independence might have worked before, but it won't now. The myths of "get rich quick" schemes that involve no work and exuberant lifestyles are unrealistic and probably gone (or at least they should be), but real opportunity for learning, growing, participating, and investment success does exist. There is a lot of capital chasing yield right now and a real shortage of safe alternative investments. In the words of Warren Buffett: "Be fearful when others are greedy and greedy when others are fearful."

If you really want investment traction and success with sustainable results over the long term, make sure you're not working against yourself. If you're only investing in liquid (current) assets, without a real understanding of what you're doing (with real information you trust), or making almost no return, or buying at the top, selling at the bottom, and repeating the process, you're working against yourself. It's estimated that 75% of non-home real estate investments in the United States are owned by the top 10% of the wealthiest individuals. Ask yourself why they would do that and everyone else doesn't. Which group would you rather be in? These individuals are not working against themselves, so why should you? Set *your* goal and pursue your dream. Map out how your goal and strategy fit into effective life leadership and that life line you drew for yourself in Chapter 2. Write it down for future reference.

To take advantage of investment opportunities, you need discipline and tools. Spending less than you make (thus being liquid), knowing what to look for in an investment property and actually looking, making financial decisions based on rigorous quantitative analysis, and becoming a good manager: these are your tools. Due diligence (measure twice, cut once) is your tool box. Follow the financial analysis advice in Chapter 4 carefully. Computers now make this kind of analysis very easy. Finding the right numbers to use in your analysis is the hard part and becoming harder all the time. Choose wisely. As Reagan often said: "Trust, but verify."

You can become a successful real estate investor, but that first step will always be saving and making that first non-home real estate investment. Many ordinary people have done so. What it demands is determination, attention to detail, hard work, the willingness to take that calculated risk, the vision to recognize windows of opportunity, and the ability to learn from your mistakes. You're probably doing a lot of this at work already. But maybe not enough of your work is actually for *you*. Now is the time to invest in yourself. You can do this. When you do, you can fill the next chapter in this book with your own story. All we ask is that you make it a great one.

"A journey of a thousand miles begins with a single step."

CONFUCIUS

Glossary

Opinionated, Common-Sense Definitions And Suggestions

A day late and a dollar short ... a pretty common excuse.

Annuity ... any recurring payment can be considered an annuity, such as Social Security payments, payments on a contract, or rental income from an investment property that is paid off. According to an article in the *Wall Street Journal* (December 17, 2010), saving enough to purchase an annuity with annual increases to replace Social Security income is a virtual impossibility for "most" Americans. Isn't it odd then that "most" Americans can figure out how to buy a home, which becomes their best investment, yet will spend the rest of their lives unable or unwilling to buy a second one, which would provide an annuity income for the rest of their lives (i.e., retirement)?

Asset Allocation ... basically the idea of not keeping one's eggs all in one basket. Investing in different asset classes reduces the risk of unacceptable loss by spreading the risk across uncorrelated

149

investments. Just because one investment does poorly, the other may still do fine, thereby balancing your return. However, the term is usually only used for making investments in liquid assets. The investments are allocated only between similar, and usually current, assets. Two problems with this type of asset allocation are:

> *First*, as history indicates, most Americans will never get enough assets to realistically generate income sufficient for anything close to what they will eventually need for financial independence.

> *Second*, the evidence of a beginning investor's success shows no real long-term proof of benefit for active secondary management of their investments (maybe because of fees). Look no further than the hedge funds of 2006 that were routinely charging 2-20. That means they were taking 2% for management and 20% of your gains as a bonus. Most of those hedge funds are gone now, along with much of their client's money. In addition, turning over all responsibility for your investment success may leave you with no real money management skills of your own.

Our central argument of this book is about "life leadership" and asset allocation for diversification into fixed asset investments (small income property being an easy, entry-level example) for an improved and balanced long-term result, as well as the development of real management skills.

Capitalization Rate ... the ratio of Net Operating Income (NOI) to what you are paying for the property (NOI / Purchase Price). This is a market-driven number, so you have two problems with it. First, is it competitive with the going rate for similar properties in the area? Second, is it accurate?

Cash On Cash Return ... The annual ratio between the Net Operating Income (NOI) less the debt service and the cash invested in the property:

NOI – DEBT SERVICE / INVESTED CASH = CASH ON CASH RETURN

Don't be surprised if there is little to no cash on cash return. When you're starting, it's not likely you're going to be hitting home runs—try for singles and get on base. Be very careful with debt, but don't be surprised if you have to feed the property. Just make sure it easily fits into your budget, and look at the negative cash flow as a forced savings plan, or dollar cost averaging with real estate that is being used to buy an annuity (see Annuity). In fact, one competitive advantage you may have starting out is your willingness to look at properties that need work and have small negative cash flows that can be fixed and made positive.

Cognitive Dissonance ... what often happens because it's easier to change our mind than our behavior. Cognitive dissonance can be explained as the emotional discomfort of having made a decision and being left with feelings of uncertainty and buyer's remorse (or even sour grapes). Cognitive dissonance is reduced after a decision by positive evidence that the correct decision was made. Likewise it is increased if there is negative evidence about the decision and will be rationalized by justification or behavioral change. Remember: It's always easier to change liquid assets than it is to change fixed assets, and that may be your one good reason why it's not always a good thing to only invest in liquid assets.

Collateralized Debt Obligation (CDO) ... a generic term for a form of asset-backed securities—including Collateralized Mortgage Obligations (CMOs)—that pass payments through from a class of assets, such as residential mortgages, often with enhanced yields, to comparably rated securities. These are terms to remember for investments that were "too good to be true" but were often marketed as extremely safe. In many cases, they were insured and guaranteed to enhance their creditworthiness as sound investments. In 2006, the subprime-mortgage-backed CDOs/CMOs became a causal element in the mortgage crisis and collapse of the housing market in the U.S. In 2007, the housing bubble finally burst because the underlying assets proved to be worth far less than advertised, forcing many insurers and guarantors to file for bankruptcy. CDOs became one of the best examples ever of investors being taught (sold) what to think instead of how to think. Stories now exist around the world about individual retail investors who lost much of what they had saved for their entire lives on an investment in a "collateralized debt obligation CDO" that they never fully understood, where "collateral" and "obligation" were at best exaggerated or at worst never actually existed. Hopefully the "Next Generation" will remember that if it's about "your money" and it seems too good to be true ... it is. As Warren Buffet predicted, CDOs were the "financial weapons of mass destruction."

Debt Service Ratio ... the debt service, or coverage, ratio is the ratio between the annual NOI and the annual debt service (NOI / Debt Service). This is a widely used measure to determine that the income from your property is sufficient to pay the mortgage payments, so leave yourself some room and cash flow. If this ratio is less than 1, then you have a negative cash flow and most responsible lenders won't/shouldn't make this loan. What's the solution? Put more cash down to lower the mortgage payments or get the seller to lower the price. Once you get the income up, you can refinance and get some or all of your cash out.

Depreciation ... an important consideration when investing in income property. The idea is that you are allowed to expense out over the life of the rental property the cost of the property for a period of 27.5 years. The reality is that for the most part any property in good condition and in a good area will in fact appreciate over those years giving the owner a source of extra cash. There is considerable disagreement over this in academia but the fact of the matter is that if the property appreciates and you save money on taxes at the same time then depreciation is a source of cash and you need to know what it is because it's part of your return on the investment.

Due Diligence ... the process of evaluating everything possible about your potential income property investment: not just the price, income and expenses, but answering questions about everything from zoning to title insurance, deferred maintenance, structural defects, building code violations, future repair costs and environmental concerns, just to name some of what due diligence means for you. We almost bought an apartment building that was on the site of an old gas station with buried gas tanks ... big problem and definitely a "deal killer" unless that cleanup is priced in. Investors commonly buy rental houses only to find old, buried oil tanks that they become responsible for. Due diligence means measure twice, cut once.

Enronian ... our term for incompetent, corrupt managers like those at Enron, the company that went bankrupt in 2001, losing billions of dollars of shareholders' money. Managers deserving this title and at this level seldom go down without taking many others with them. Imagine your investment of your life savings going from $90 a share to less than $1 in under a year. Then imagine anyone dumb enough not to learn anything from this ... that's Enronian.

Financial Independence ... the point in your financial life where your money is finally working for you. Your income from your investments has surpassed your income from working and freed you from the financial necessity to work. Many people like their work and will keep at it long after they don't need to just because they find it rewarding, but it's truly nice to not have to.

Future Value ... (FV) is the value of a dollar at some point in the future. It can easily be calculated if you know how far in the future and the interest, or growth, rate. Likewise, any future value can be discounted to what is called a **Present value** (PV). This works for single amounts as well as annuities or combinations of the two. Often these are used on expected or anticipated values and returns to evaluate investment proposals. Be cautious here because these are usually hypothetical numbers being used to create real expectations.

Good Investments ... what many miss while waiting for great investments, not realizing that *good* is often on the way to *great*. They may have only needed good but wanted great. Make sure you get what you really need before you ignore it to wait for what you think you want. When our expectations are set for *great*, we may often feel cheated when only offered *good*. Sadly, many don't recognize that no one truly great at anything got there before they were good.

Inflation ... is generally considered to be a rise in the aggregate level of prices. There is common agreement that one cause of high inflation is printing money or, put another way, the unreasonable increase in the money supply. Since 2008 the U.S. Federal Reserve has significantly increased its printing of money. So how's this affecting you? Well, let's look at a fixed asset like real estate. According to the U.S. Census Bureau, the median home value in 1940 was $2,938; it was $17,000 by 1970, about a 479% increase. If we look ahead another 30 years to the year 2000, it was $119,600, which is an additional 604% increase. That means during each of the last two 30-year periods in the U.S., home prices rose over 450%. That's a 60-year period when there wasn't nearly as much money being printed as there is now. Question: Has anything happened recently to make us think inflation might be less in the next 30-year period?

The government also manages the math and consistently changes the way it calculates inflation to make it look like the government is doing a better job. It's called the inflation adjusted price. Of course you pay the "actual price," not the inflation adjusted price.

Look at the way the measurement of the Consumer Price Index (CPI) has been changed. Look up "hedonics" and see how it's used in measuring the CPI. You don't really believe the things you're buying are only going up in price by 1%–2% a year, do you? Imagine what would happen to the value of your liquid investments during high inflation (like 10% or higher), and you'll see why investing (now) in something tangible with intrinsic value, like real estate, is probably a reasonable idea.

Insanity ... "Doing the same thing over and over again and expecting different results."—Albert Einstein

Internal Rate of Return (IRR) ... not the best measure of return when you're starting out, primarily because you don't really know what the holding period will be for your property, and secondly because if everything else in your analysis looks good the IRR is going to look great. IRR is that interest rate that equates the cash inflows with the cash outflows ... better be good since you put in all the numbers it's based on!

Liar's Loans ... loans made without any documentation or verification of the information supplied by a buyer. Another common term for this is "ninja loan," meaning the buyer had "No income, No job, No assets" but they still got the loan! Then came the mortgage crisis, income documentation, no more flipping, and they lost their houses.

Liquidity ... a general measure of how easily an asset can be converted to cash to meet current obligations. In business, this is a common measure of a business's financial well-being. The problem of liquidity, when it comes to individuals, is that too often everything is liquid and everything is lost or spent (as we are unfortunately seeing in this current financial crisis). In business, a common ratio used to measure a reasonable amount of liquidity is called the "current ratio," which is the ratio of cash (or cash-like assets) to current obligations. As long as the company can easily meet its current obligations, it's free to invest in less liquid assets that will have a higher return and help magnify the profit of the company, which is its responsibility to the owners/shareholders. We have this same obligation to ourselves and families—to have safe and sufficient liquid assets but also to invest in less liquid assets that will help ensure our future success.

Loan-To-Value Ratio (LTV) ... another common ratio used to determine your equity or risk capital invested in a property. In general, LTV is the amount of the loan divided by the price or appraised value of the property. Don't be surprised if you need as much as 25%–30% down on property that is being used for investment purposes. Often any property under four units isn't considered commercial property and may qualify for a better interest rate or lower down payment, so don't hesitate to shop for these rates.

Net Operating Income (NOI) ... the income on your property after vacancy, losses and expenses. Before you buy the property, this is just a projection; after the purchase is closed, it becomes an expectation. We recommend you carefully revisit NOI when estimating your underlying expectations about income and expenses. Do this before you buy any income property.

Offering Price Elasticity ... the amount of wiggle room or variance you have between the seller's offering price and what they will actually take for the property. This elasticity also includes the variance in the terms and time as components of the price. Use them all wisely.

Profit ... for our purposes here, profit is what you are hoping to gain on a sale over what you paid to acquire a given investment. The point about profit is that it is a much more difficult calculation to arrive at for fixed assets as compared to liquid assets because of differing laws, tax considerations, and methods available for valuations ... just to name a few. There are, however, advantages to investments in fixed assets (like small income-producing properties) that can make it more than worth the difficulty. You might want to think of these advantages as invisible income or benefits to owning. Liquid assets have the advantage of just that ... being liquid (i.e., easily convertible to cash). Fixed assets have all the advantages we've discussed in this book, such as depreciation, which may be a source of cash. We suggest you take all the advantages of both and manage your profit.

Rules Of Thumb ... generalizations that have a basis in fact that can increase your comfort level with a possible purchase but can also lead to hasty decisions and bad outcomes when not combined with a disciplined approach to an analysis.

Examples:

- When looking at small income properties, the income is (or should be) at least 1% of the purchase price. This will help you get a ballpark idea of where to come in with an offer.
- Be at least the third owner ... a rule of thumb to lower your risk on a property purchase. Some believe the first owner/developer is often in too deep and will lose the property because of optimistic projections. This means you buy from the lender that has taken it back from a developer, making you the third owner.
- Location, location, location ... this is a good one.

Under Contract ... this term means different things in different places and different things to different people. Usually it means there is an accepted offer in good faith by a willing seller and a willing buyer on a property with contingencies still to work out, but it doesn't mean the deal is done. At best it means there is an ongoing negotiation on the property that technically continues right up to the moment it closes. It could mean the seller accepted an offer an hour ago or that the deal has been smoothly progressing and will close today. The point being that if you are really interested in a particular property and have been told it's under contract, don't hesitate to ask for details and express your interest in improving the offer. Just be sure to leave your contact information. It's not at all unusual for a deal that's under contract to fall through and go to the next in line. A word of caution to the buyer: Don't get bullied during negotiations once you're under contract, but don't over-negotiate and lose a property you might have been smart to own.

Vacancy Rate ... a good measure of how you are treating your tenants and managing your property. If you don't think your tenants are your partners in the success of this venture, see how you feel when it's empty for a while.

Appendix

Pro Forma Property Analysis Template and Samples

After you answer the questions about the property analysis assumptions (see pp. 94–95), and you're confident they are accurate, you are ready to analyze an income property investment of your own. We've included a blank analysis template, followed by an example analysis of a duplex, four-plex and eight-plex.

A printable version of the blank templates featured here is available for download at www.TheSustainableInvestment.com. The document password is retsi.

We recommend using the blank template by hand at least once. Then you may want to enter it into a portable (easy to share by email) spreadsheet program, such as Excel, with built-in financial functions for amortization and appreciation. Be sure the amortization schedule in your spreadsheet matches the amortization schedule of the actual loan on the property you're considering. Also, if the box in the analysis is shaded, it's what you need to "find" out. If it's not shaded, it's what you need to "figure" out!

This information is for educational purposes only and is considered accurate and authoritative; however, the authors are not rendering legal, accounting or any other professional services and recommend always seeking competent legal and accounting services on any real estate transaction.

Pro Forma Property Analysis Template - Part 1 (input)

Type of Property:
Location:

	Number of Units	Projected monthly rent / unit
Total Units		
2 Bdrm Units		
1 Bdrm Units		
Other units		

Projected annual rental income:
Other annual income (Laundry, Fees, etc.):
Scheduled Gross Income

Description of Facts

Asking Price: Land:
Improvements: Salvage Value:
Asking Price / Unit:

Rentable Sq. Footage:

Depreciation Method: Depreciation / year:

Proposed Financing

Amount: N (years) =
Interest Rate: Annual Payments:
                                 Monthly Payments:

Property Income Statement
Scheduled Gross Income
(% Vacancy & Credit Losses)

Gross Operating Income

Less: Operating Expenses
Property Taxes
Insurance
Utilities
Licenses / Permits
Advertising
Management
Payroll
Supplies
Administrative
Maintenance
Replacement Reserve

Total Operating Expenses

Net Operating Income

Capitalization Rate
(Net Operating Income / Market Value)

Comments:

These examples and calculations are for illustrative purposes only, and do not reflect actual properties, market values, loans, operating income or expenses.

Pro Forma Property Analysis Template - Part 2 (results)

	Year 1	Year 5	Year 10
Equity Calculation			
Market Value (Beg)			
Less: Total Loans			
Owner's Equity			
Tax Calculation			
Net Operating Income			
Less: Interest			
Less: Depreciation			
Taxable Income			
Income Tax			
Income Tax Rate			
Cash Flow Calculation			
Net Operating Income			
Less: Financing Pmts			
Gross Spendable			
Less: Income Tax			
Net Spendable			
Net Spendable Rate			
(Net Spendable / Equity)			
Equity Income			
Net Spendable			
Plus: Principal Reduction			
Plus: Market Value Growth			
Net Equity Income			
Net Equity Income Rate			
(Net Equity Income / Equity)			

FYI: Accumulative Market Value Growth

FYI: Total Interest Paid (accumulative)

FYI: Accumulative Gross Operating Income

Notes on Growth Projections:

*Assumed Gross Operating Income % increase by year =

*Assumed Total Operating Expenses % increase by year =

*Assumed % growth in market value by year =

Year 15	Year 20	Year 25	Year 30

Pro Forma Property Analysis - Duplex - Part 1 (input)

Type of Property:	Your next rental property could be a duplex	
Location:	Hopefully in a really good location	

	Number of Units	Projected monthly rent / unit
Total Units	2	$1,400
2 Bdrm Units	2	$700
1 Bdrm Units	0	$0
Other units	0	$0

Projected annual rental income:	$16,800
Other annual income (Laundry, Fees, etc.):	$0
Scheduled Gross Income	$16,800

Description of Facts

Asking Price:	$239,000	**Land:**	$39,000
Improvements:	$200,000	**Salvage Value:**	0
Asking Price / Unit:	$119,500		

Rentable Sq. Footage:	1500

Depreciation Method:	27.5 years	**Depreciation / year:**	$7,272.73

Proposed Financing

Amount:	$200,000	**N =**	30
Interest Rate:	6.00%	**Annual Payments:**	($14,389)
		Monthly Payments:	($1,199)

Property Income Statement

Scheduled Gross Income		16,800
(% Vacancy & Credit Losses)	6%	(1,008)
Gross Operating Income		**15,792**
Less: Operating Expenses		
Property Taxes		3,400
Insurance		700
Utilities		-
Licenses / Permits		-
Advertising		-
Management		1,200
Payroll		-
Supplies		-
Administrative		
Maintenance		2,200
Replacement Reserve		500
Total Operating Expenses		**8,000**
Net Operating Income		**7,792**
Capitalization Rate		**0.033**
(Net Operating Income / Market Value)		

Comments:

These examples and calculations are for illustrative purposes only,
and do not reflect actual properties, market values, loans,
operating income or expenses.

Pro Forma Property Analysis - Duplex - Part 2 (results)

	Year 1	Year 5	Year 10
Equity Calculation			
Market Value (Beg)	239,000	290,506	370,767
Less: Total Loans	200,000	189,229	171,580
Owner's Equity	**39,000**	**101,277**	**199,187**
Tax Calculation			
Net Operating Income	7,792	9,470	12,039
Less: Interest	11,933	11,269	10,180
Less: Depreciation	7,273	7,273	7,273
Taxable Income	**(11,414)**	**(9,071)**	**(5,414)**
Income Tax	**(3,995)**	**(3,175)**	**(1,895)**
Income Tax Rate	0.35	0.35	0.35
Cash Flow Calculation			
Net Operating Income	7,792	9,470	12,039
Less: Financing Pmts	(14,389)	(14,389)	(14,389)
Gross Spendable	**(6,597)**	**(4,919)**	**(2,350)**
Less: Income Tax	(3,995)	(3,175)	(1,895)
Net Spendable	**(2,602)**	**(1,744)**	**(455)**
Net Spendable Rate	**(0.067)**	**(0.045)**	**(0.012)**
(Net Spendable / Equity)			
Equity Income			
Net Spendable	(2,602)	(1,744)	(455)
Plus: Principal Reduction	2,456	3,120	4,209
Plus: Market Value Growth	-	13,834	17,656
Net Equity Income	**(146)**	**15,210**	**21,409**
Net Equity Income Rate	**(0.004)**	**0.390**	**0.549**
(Net Equity Income / Equity)			
FYI: Accumulative Market Value Growth	_-_	_51,506_	_131,767_
FYI: Total Interest Paid (accumulative)	_11,933_	_58,055_	_111,264_
FYI: Accumulative Gross Operating Incom	_15,792_	_85,535_	_189,600_

Notes on Growth Projections:

*Assumed Gross Operating Income % increase by year =	4%
*Assumed Total Operating Expenses % increase by year =	3%
*Assumed % growth in market value by year =	5%

Year 15	Year 20	Year 25	Year 30
473,204	603,941	770,799	983,756
147,775	115,665	72,353	13,932
325,429	**488,276**	**698,446**	**969,824**
15,246	19,243	24,217	30,397
8,712	6,732	4,060	457
7,273	7,273	7,273	-
(739)	**5,239**	**12,884**	**29,940**
(259)	**1,834**	**4,510**	**10,479**
0.35	0.35	0.35	0.35
15,246	19,243	24,217	30,397
(14,389)	(14,389)	(14,389)	(14,389)
857	**4,854**	**9,828**	**16,008**
(259)	1,834	4,510	10,479
1,115	**3,020**	**5,319**	**5,529**
0.029	**0.077**	**0.136**	**0.142**
1,115	3,020	5,319	5,529
5,677	7,658	10,329	13,932
22,534	28,759	36,705	46,846
29,326	**39,437**	**52,352**	**66,307**
0.752	**1.011**	**1.342**	**1.700**
234,204	*364,941*	*531,799*	*744,756*
157,936	*195,791*	*221,754*	*231,676*
316,212	*470,255*	*657,672*	*885,693*

Pro Forma Property Analysis - Four-Plex - Part 1 (input)

| Type of Property: | A Fourplex is next.... |
| Location: | Are you ready? |

	Number of Units	Projected monthly rent / unit
Total Units	4	$2,800
2 Bdrm Units	4	$700
1 Bdrm Units	0	$0
Other units	0	$0

Projected annual rental income:	$33,600
Other annual income (Laundry, Fees, etc.):	$0
Scheduled Gross Income	$33,600

Description of Facts

Asking Price:	$350,000	Land:	$50,000
Improvements:	$300,000	Salvage Value:	0
Asking Price / Unit:	$87,500		

Rentable Sq. Footage:	3000

Depreciation Method:	27.5 years	Depreciation / year:	$10,909.09

Proposed Financing

Amount:	$300,000	N =	30
Interest Rate:	6.00%	Annual Payments:	($21,584)
		Monthly Payments:	($1,799)

Property Income Statement

Scheduled Gross Income		33,600
(% Vacancy & Credit Losses)	6%	(2,016)
Gross Operating Income		**31,584**

Less: Operating Expenses

Property Taxes	3,626
Insurance	650
Utilities	1,750
Licenses / Permits	-
Advertising	-
Management	2,400
Payroll	-
Supplies	-
Administrative	500
Maintenance	2,500
Replacement Reserve	1,500

Total Operating Expenses	**12,926**
Net Operating Income	**18,658**

Capitalization Rate   **0.053**
(Net Operating Income / Market Value)

Comments:

These examples and calculations are for illustrative purposes only,
and do not reflect actual properties, market values, loans,
operating income or expenses.

Pro Forma Property Analysis - Four-Plex - Part 2 (results)

	Year 1	Year 5	Year 10
Equity Calculation			
Market Value (Beg)	350,000	425,427	542,965
Less: Total Loans	300,000	283,844	257,371
Owner's Equity	50,000	141,584	285,594
Tax Calculation			
Net Operating Income	18,658	22,400	28,088
Less: Interest	17,900	16,903	15,270
Less: Depreciation	10,909	10,909	10,909
Taxable Income	(10,151)	(5,412)	1,909
Income Tax	(3,553)	(1,894)	668
Income Tax Rate	0.35	0.35	0.35
Cash Flow Calculation			
Net Operating Income	18,658	22,400	28,088
Less: Financing Pmts	(21,584)	(21,584)	(21,584)
Gross Spendable	(2,926)	817	6,505
Less: Income Tax	(3,553)	(1,894)	668
Net Spendable	627	2,711	5,836
Net Spendable Rate	0.013	0.054	0.117
(Net Spendable / Equity)			
Equity Income			
Net Spendable	627	2,711	5,836
Plus: Principal Reduction	3,684	4,681	6,313
Plus: Market Value Growth	-	20,258	25,855
Net Equity Income	4,311	27,650	38,005
Net Equity Income Rate	0.086	0.553	0.760
(Net Equity Income / Equity)			
FYI: Accumulative Market Value Growth	-	75,427	192,965
FYI: Total Interest Paid (accumulative)	17,900	87,082	166,895
FYI: Accumulative Gross Operating Income	31,584	171,069	379,201

Notes on Growth Projections:

*Assumed Gross Operating Income % increase by year = 4%

*Assumed Total Operating Expenses % increase by year = 3%

*Assumed % growth in market value by year = 5%

Year 15	Year 20	Year 25	Year 30
692,976	884,433	1,128,785	1,440,647
221,662	173,497	108,530	20,898
471,314	**710,935**	**1,020,255**	**1,419,749**
35,142	43,877	54,684	68,039
13,068	10,097	6,090	685
10,909	10,909	10,909	-
11,164	**22,870**	**37,684**	**67,353**
3,908	**8,005**	**13,189**	**23,574**
0.35	0.35	0.35	0.35
35,142	43,877	54,684	68,039
(21,584)	(21,584)	(21,584)	(21,584)
13,558	**22,293**	**33,100**	**46,455**
3,908	8,005	13,189	23,574
9,650	**14,288**	**19,910**	**22,881**
0.193	**0.286**	**0.398**	**0.458**
9,650	14,288	19,910	22,881
8,516	11,486	15,494	20,898
32,999	42,116	53,752	68,602
51,165	**67,891**	**89,155**	**112,382**
1.023	**1.358**	**1.783**	**2.248**
342,976	*534,433*	*778,785*	*1,090,647*
236,904	*293,687*	*332,632*	*347,515*
632,425	*940,511*	*1,315,344*	*1,771,387*

Pro Forma Property Analysis - Eight-Plex - Part 1 (input)

Type of Property:	Eight-Plex	
Location:	This is a step up ... Be careful, all your mistakes are times 8!	

	Number of Units	Projected monthly rent / unit
Total Units	8	$5,600
2 Bdrm Units	8	$700
1 Bdrm Units	0	$0
Other units	0	$0

Projected annual rental income:	$67,200
Other annual income (Laundry, Fees, etc.):	$1,200
Scheduled Gross Income	**$68,400**

Description of Facts

Asking Price:	$560,000	**Land:**	$50,000
Improvements:	$510,000	**Salvage Value:**	0
Asking Price / Unit:	$70,000		

Rentable Sq. Footage:	5600

Depreciation Method:	27.5 years	**Depreciation / year:**	$18,545.45

Proposed Financing

Amount:	$420,000	**N =**	30
Interest Rate:	6.00%	**Annual Payments:**	($30,217)
		Monthly Payments:	($2,518)

Property Income Statement

Scheduled Gross Income		68,400
(% Vacancy & Credit Losses)	6%	(4,104)
Gross Operating Income		**64,296**
Less: Operating Expenses		
Property Taxes		5,300
Insurance		2,100
Utilities		3,500
Licenses / Permits		-
Advertising		-
Management		4,800
Payroll		-
Supplies		-
Administrative		2,400
Maintenance		9,600
Replacement Reserve		1,500
Total Operating Expenses		**29,200**
Net Operating Income		**35,096**
Capitalization Rate		**0.063**
(Net Operating Income / Market Value)		

Comments:

These examples and calculations are for illustrative purposes only,
and do not reflect actual properties, market values, loans,
operating income or expenses.

Pro Forma Property Analysis - Eight-Plex - Part 2 (results)

	Year 1	Year 5	Year 10
Equity Calculation			
Market Value (Beg)	560,000	680,684	868,744
Less: Total Loans	420,000	397,381	360,319
Owner's Equity	**140,000**	**283,302**	**508,425**
Tax Calculation			
Net Operating Income	35,096	42,352	53,414
Less: Interest	25,060	23,665	21,379
Less: Depreciation	18,545	18,545	18,545
Taxable Income	**(8,509)**	**142**	**13,490**
Income Tax	**(2,978)**	**50**	**4,721**
Income Tax Rate	0.35	0.35	0.35
Cash Flow Calculation			
Net Operating Income	35,096	42,352	53,414
Less: Financing Pmts	(30,217)	(30,217)	(30,217)
Gross Spendable	**4,879**	**12,135**	**23,197**
Less: Income Tax	(2,978)	50	4,721
Net Spendable	**7,857**	**12,085**	**18,475**
Net Spendable Rate	**0.056**	**0.086**	**0.132**
(Net Spendable / Equity)			
Equity Income			
Net Spendable	7,857	12,085	18,475
Plus: Principal Reduction	5,158	6,553	8,839
Plus: Market Value Growth	-	32,414	41,369
Net Equity Income	**13,015**	**51,051**	**68,683**
Net Equity Income Rate	**0.093**	**0.365**	**0.491**
(Net Equity Income / Equity)			
FYI: Accumulative Market Value Growth	-	*120,684*	*308,744*
FYI: Total Interest Paid (accumulative)	*25,060*	*121,915*	*233,654*
FYI: Accumulative Gross Operating Income	*64,296*	*348,248*	*771,945*

Notes on Growth Projections:

*Assumed Gross Operating Income % increase by year =	4%
*Assumed Total Operating Expenses % increase by year =	3%
*Assumed % growth in market value by year =	5%

Year 15	Year 20	Year 25	Year 30
1,108,762	1,415,092	1,806,056	2,305,036
310,327	242,896	151,942	29,258
798,435	**1,172,196**	**1,654,114**	**2,275,778**
67,172	84,260	105,453	131,705
18,295	14,136	8,526	960
18,545	18,545	18,545	-
30,331	**51,578**	**78,381**	**130,746**
10,616	**18,052**	**27,433**	**45,761**
0.35	0.35	0.35	0.35
67,172	84,260	105,453	131,705
(30,217)	(30,217)	(30,217)	(30,217)
36,955	**54,042**	**75,235**	**101,488**
10,616	18,052	27,433	45,761
26,339	**35,990**	**47,802**	**55,727**
0.188	**0.257**	**0.341**	**0.398**
26,339	35,990	47,802	55,727
11,922	16,081	21,691	29,258
52,798	67,385	86,003	109,764
91,059	**119,456**	**155,496**	**194,748**
0.650	**0.853**	**1.111**	**1.391**
548,762	*855,092*	*1,246,056*	*1,745,036*
331,665	*411,162*	*465,684*	*486,520*
1,287,437	*1,914,611*	*2,677,665*	*3,606,037*

Further Reading

Investing in Real Estate by G. Eldred, John Wiley & Sons, 2003.

The Wall Street Journal. Complete Real-Estate Investing Guidebook by D. Crook, Three Rivers Press, 2006.

Real Estate Finance and Investments by W. Brueggeman and J. Fisher, McGraw-Hill Higher Education, 2010.

Real Estate Principles: A Value Approach by D. Ling and W. Archer, Irwin Pro, 2004.

Real Estate 101: Building Wealth With Real Estate Investments, by G. Eldred, Trump University, John Wiley & Sons, 2009.

Real Estate by A. Ring, J. Shilling and J. Dasso, South-Western Education Pub, 2001.

The Complete Guide to Investing in Rental Properties by S. Berges, McGraw-Hill, 2004.

What Every Real Estate Investor Needs To Know About Cash Flow … and 36 Other Key Financial Measures by F. Gallinelli, McGraw-Hill, 2003.

Dictionary of Real Estate Terms by J. Friedman, J. Harris, and J. Lindeman, 7th Edition, Barron's, 2008.

Online Resources

www.thesustainableinvestment.com
The publisher's website, where you can download a copy of our Pro Forma Property Analysis sheets (password: retsi). We highly recommend reading the book before you use them.

www.craigslist.com
Great for finding properties for sale all over the world and also really good for advertising your vacancies.

www.findlaw.com
Useful legal information.

www.zillow.com
Great site to see comparable values in the area you're interested in.

www.housingmaps.com
Craigslist meets Google Maps.

www.loopnet.com
Great source for investment property listings.

About the Authors

GLEN R. SWEENEY is a real estate investor and Managing Partner for a number of real estate investment partnerships. He is the President of Investors Research Institute, Inc. (IRI) and has established real estate investment and development LLCs with a wide variety of partners. He has also been a management consultant to major forest products companies on divestiture issues, marketing analysis and corporate reorganization. He has taught Finance and Operations Management at Oregon State University's College of Business and been an adjunct professor of Finance and Investments at Linfield College. He has been an invited lecturer at Yale, Oxford, University of Munich and Portland State University. He began his higher education at New York University and holds an MBA from Oregon State University. He is also the author of a curriculum on capital budgeting.

JOHN C. GORDON has invested in rental, forest and farm real estate for over 30 years. He is Pinchot Professor of Forestry and Environmental Studies Emeritus at the Yale School of Forestry and Environmental Studies, and was Dean at Yale Forestry from 1983 to 1992 and again in 1997/98. He holds a Ph.D. from Iowa State University and has been a Fulbright Scholar in Finland (University of Helsinki) and India (Bangalore). He has extensive consulting experience with public and private organizations, including leading natural resource and land holding firms. He has authored or coauthored over 100 publications, including books on investing and leadership. He is a managing partner in Candlewood Timber Group, LLC, and Maximum Yield Associates, LLC.

Made in the USA
Charleston, SC
27 August 2011